GENERATION

GENERATION

by WILLIAM GOODHART

1966

DOUBLEDAY & COMPANY, INC., GARDEN CITY, N.Y.

Photographs courtesy of Eileen Darby, Graphic House, Inc.

For Joanne

GENERATION was first presented by Frederick Brisson at the Morosco Theatre, New York City, on October 6, 1965, with the following cast:

Walter Owen	Richard Jordan
Jim Bolton	Henry Fonda
Doris Owen	Holly Turner
Stan Herman	A. Larry Haines
Winston Garand	Don Fellows
Ken Powell	Sandy Baron

Directed by Gene Saks

Incidental Music by Jerry Bock

Lyrics by William Goodhart

Scenery and Lighting by George Jenkins

Costumes by Albert Wolsky

CAST OF CHARACTERS

(In order of appearance)

WALTER OWEN

JIM BOLTON

DORIS OWEN

STAN HERMAN

WINSTON GARAND

KEN POWELL

The play takes place in the studio-loft apartment of Walter Owen, in Lower Manhattan

Time: The present

ACT I

Late Saturday afternoon

ACT II

Sunday afternoon

ACT III

That evening

ACT I

SCENE: *A studio apartment has been built into a large, light, high-ceilinged loft, located on the second floor of an old industrial building in Lower Manhattan. The brick walls and the beamed ceiling are painted white, the floor and the furniture are natural wood tones, and the large sheet of photographer's background paper, which hangs down against the back wall, is a delicate sky blue.*

There is a minimum of furniture, most of it built in along the walls. On one side is a studio couch, a bookcase full of paperbacks, and a small desk, and on the other, a simple kitchen is lined up against the wall. Downstage center there is a round pedestal table and three low stools. The entire upstage area is kept clear for picture-taking, although the only photographic equipment visible is a couple of light stands.

On the kitchen side, a homemade partition, built of plywood, juts out from the side wall and runs up to the back wall. The room thus enclosed is entered by a door in the downstage section of the partition. Up by the back wall, another door leads to an offstage part of the loft, and a third door, a heavy, metal-clad fire door, downstage in the side wall, leads out into a decrepit old hallway and stair well.

On the opposite side of the room is an expanse of large plate-glass windows which afford a view of other old loft buildings across the street, and admit the last rays of the late afternoon sunlight.

1

Despite the industrial character of the building, the place has a clean, uncluttered, whitewashed look, sparse and austere as an old Shaker meeting house.

At rise: WALTER OWEN *enters through the front door carrying a handsome overnight bag. He is in his twenties, about six feet tall, with a pleasant but rather intense face and slightly long hair. He wears an old tweed sport jacket, green chinos, and a blue work shirt dressed up with a black knit tie.* WALTER *is a complicated young man who takes himself very seriously, and finds this fact amusing.*

WALTER. (*Calling into the loft as he enters*) Dorrie! Your father's here! (*He drops the bag and starts looking around for her*) Dorrie!

(JIM BOLTON *enters. He is forty-eight, vigorous, hearty, and, judging from his appearance, very successful. Yet there is something vaguely desperate in his manner; his smile is a little too eager, his laughter is too quick, and his efforts to gain approval are a bit too obvious. He has two dollar bills in his hand.*)

(WALTER *opens the door in the partition and calls into the room*)

Doris!

BOLTON. Isn't she here?

WALTER. I guess not . . . She must have gone out for something.

BOLTON. (*Disappointed, his smile fades*) Oh . . . (*He quickly becomes enthusiastic about the studio*) Hey! This is a really marvelous place you have here!

WALTER. Thank you.

BOLTON. Boy, this is great. I see what you meant about space! Yes sir, this is really great! There's a wonderful *honest* feeling about it! It's so simple yet it has atmosphere. (*Looks out window*) When you look out here, you really get the feeling of, uh, Lower Manhattan.

WALTER. I'm sorry Doris isn't here to get your reaction.

BOLTON. Well I'll react again for her. (*Laughs and then asks with a note of concern*) Where do you think she is?

WALTER. (*Concealing his own concern*) She must be down at the grocery store getting something for dinner.

BOLTON. Oh well, actually I planned to take you out for a sort of belated wedding dinner, or something. I thought you'd probably know of some marvelous little place down here with great food that the tourists haven't discovered yet.

WALTER. Yeah, well I haven't discovered it yet either. Don't you want to eat here?

BOLTON. Oh sure! Of course! I'd love it! I see you have a stove and everything. That's wonderful. It never occurred to me that Doris could cook.

WALTER. I taught her how.

BOLTON. (*After the slightest hesitation, exclaims jovially*)
Oh good, good! (*He becomes aware of the money in his
hand*) Listen, will you please take this cab fare?

WALTER. (*Pretending not to hear, he crosses to window*)
Yeah, she must be down at the grocery.

BOLTON. (*Covers and moves around, still jovial*) Well, uh,
while we're waiting, we'll, uh, just have a drink or something.

WALTER. Oh. I'm sorry, we don't have anything. *Dammit,* I
should have thought of that!

BOLTON. Oh no, no! It doesn't matter a bit!

WALTER. No, I should have thought of that!

BOLTON. No, no, I shouldn't have even mentioned it . . . I
don't need a drink . . . (*But he obviously does want a drink
and suddenly says hopefully*) Hey, maybe that's what Doris
has gone after— Not that it matters of course!

WALTER. (*After a moment of indecision*) Uh, say, uh, I'll
take your coat.

BOLTON. (*Laughs*) You remind me of the fellow who couldn't
bring himself to call his mother-in-law "Mother," so he

4

called her "Say" until the baby was born, and then he called her "Grandmaw." Why don't you just call me "Jim." That's what my friends call me.

WALTER. I've been waiting to see what would come out *naturally*.

BOLTON. (*Suddenly feeling phony*) Oh. Sure, sure, I understand. (WALTER *turns and starts for door*) Anyway, "Say" might just fit me.

(WALTER *takes the coat into the upstage room.* BOLTON, *taking advantage of this, places the two dollars on the desk, regards it for a moment, and whipping a small notebook out of his pocket, makes a quick notation*)

WALTER. (*Returning from the room*) That trip down in the cab made me realize how absolutely rotten I am at small talk.

BOLTON. Oh, me too, me too!

WALTER. Are you kidding? You're fantastic at small talk! It just pours out of you!

BOLTON. (*Not exactly flattered*) Yeah. Well, maybe it's time we tried some big talk. (*Sits on a stool, first checking its stability*)

WALTER. Okay. (*He leans against the counter and waits*)

BOLTON. (*Suddenly finding himself on the spot*) Well, this is really a nice place. It's great to be back down here. Did Doris tell you I lived over in the Village just before the war?

WALTER. Yeah.

BOLTON. I loved it! It was the happiest time of my life! Of course, in those days, nobody lived here in this industrial area, but, uh, I suppose this isn't any worse than other neighborhoods, and once you get used to the idea of living in a loft building, and the smell of that hallway, then you, uh, have all this space . . . Now that I think of it, isn't it against the law to live in a loft building?

WALTER. I'm an A.I.R.

BOLTON. A what?

WALTER. Artist In Residence. It's a special Building Department permit for artists to live in their studios.

BOLTON. I thought you were a photographer.

WALTER. (*Ironically*) Well, there is an art of photography, you know . . . At least that's my story and I'm, uh, stuck with it. (*Smiles ruefully*)

BOLTON. Oh, of course! Certainly there is! I didn't mean to imply that you weren't artistic. Listen, if the Building Department likes your work, that's all that matters. (*He laughs.* WALTER *doesn't*) Where is that grocery store, anyway?

WALTER. (*A little tensely*) Down the street. She'll be back in a minute.

BOLTON. Oh sure! Listen, I'm enjoying our little chat. I was just wondering if, you know, maybe Doris was upset or something.

WALTER. Why?

BOLTON. Oh I don't know, here I fly all the way in from Chicago on a moment's notice, and she's not at the terminal, and then she's not here either. It's not like her, that's all. And, well, weddings sometimes upset girls . . . (*Rises, and starts to pace again*)

WALTER. It didn't upset Doris.

BOLTON. (*Quickly*) It doesn't upset me either! Actually there's no reason for Doris to avoid *me*; she knows how liberal-minded I am. But you take somebody like her mother, for example—of course she doesn't know yet, thank God—but if she were here she'd start right in beating us over the head with the Social Register or something. But Doris and I have always been very close—not that we have some Oedipus thing going. Hell, I'm *glad* she got married. You seem like a nice enough fellow.

WALTER. Thank you . . . so do you.

7

(During the following, he crosses down left to the coat rack, and taking off his jacket, hangs it up. This reveals the fact that he is wearing around his neck a bright blue necklace made of large glass beads)

BOLTON. Thank you. Of course I'll have to admit that I'm a little disappointed she didn't have a regular wedding. I've always imagined myself walking down the aisle, giving the bride away . . . *(He sees* WALTER's *necklace and stares at it in disbelief)* Well, uh, as I was saying, I wish— *(Trying not to stare at the necklace, he loses his train of thought)* What was I saying? . . . Oh, uh, the wedding— Well you know, champagne, women crying and all that . . . but I must say in my wildest dreams, I never imagined that the bridegroom would be wearing a blue necklace! *(Laughs with forced joviality)*

WALTER. Yeah, well, of course I didn't wear it at the wedding.

BOLTON. *(Still jovial)* Oh well, *that's* good.

WALTER. Naturally, I wore my *pearls* then. (BOLTON *stares*) I'm *kidding!* *(Laughs)*

BOLTON. *(Laughing uncertainly)* This is just a joke then, huh?

WALTER. *(Takes off necklace and shows it to* BOLTON) Well, uh, no, not really. I like these, actually. I came across all these great little pieces of blue glass—a friend of mine is a glassblower—and I made this necklace for Doris.

8

BOLTON. Does she ever get to wear it?

WALTER. Sure, this is the first time I've ever worn it.

BOLTON. (*Incredulously*) You mean you're wearing it in *my* honor!

WALTER. (*Thinks*) I don't think so. When I was getting up this morning, it was on the bureau, and the light was really beautiful on it. So I said to Dorrie, "Boy, this necklace is really great! I think I'll wear it today." She laughed and said, "Why not? All the primitive warriors wear them." So I decided to wear it today. (*Puts necklace back on*) I mean, if my masculinity depends on not wearing a little string of glass beads, well, you know, forget it. (*He waits for* BOLTON *to concur, but he doesn't.* WALTER *covers and goes on*) But *then*, we remembered that you were coming in today, and so here I am, up two minutes, and already I'm caught up in this *ridiculous* dilemma. (*Laughs ruefully*) I mean, it's not just you—it's been happening to me a lot lately. I get caught in these stupid hang ups.

BOLTON. Well, you shouldn't have been concerned about *my* reaction.

WALTER. Right! Having *felt* that I wanted to wear it, I had to be true to myself and wear it.

BOLTON. (*Trying hard*) Right! That's very good, Walter, I'm glad you followed through on that. It's very important to

9

be true to yourself. That's why I let Doris come to New York. You see, her mother didn't want her to come here and become a beatnik, but I sided with Doris. I guess there's still a touch of the beatnik in me too.

WALTER. She's not a beatnik.

BOLTON. Yeah, well, that is old hat, I suppose. What is she now? What's the latest?

WALTER. I don't know. Why does she have to *be* something?

BOLTON. She doesn't! I didn't mean to put a label on her or anything like that. (*Disturbed, he turns away, and his eye falls on the two dollars on the desk*) . . . Say, will you please take that taxi money, I've already written it down in my tax record!

WALTER. How come?

BOLTON. Oh, I'll have lunch with a few friends from the agency here, and deduct the whole trip as a business expense. (*He winks*) Standard procedure.

WALTER. Don't they have new rules about giving reasons and things?

BOLTON. (*Displaying the notebook*) Taxi to photographer's studio, two dollars. It all adds up, you know.

WALTER. (*Picking up* BOLTON's *bag, takes it into the upstage room, saying*) Don't forget to add a quarter for the bellhop.

(BOLTON *watches him exit, uncertain how to take this.* DORIS OWEN *enters the front door. She is an attractive girl of twenty-five, with a serene, intelligent face. She is wearing* WALTER's *raincoat, which is too big for her, and carrying a brown paper bag, which she puts on the counter*)

DORIS. (*Seeing* BOLTON) Daddy! You're here! (*They embrace*)

BOLTON. Sweetheart!

DORIS. Mmm! Oh, I'm so glad! How long have you been here?

BOLTON. Oh, just a little while. We've been getting acquainted!

DORIS. (*Crossing down right, taking off her coat*) Oh, I *knew* you'd like each other.

BOLTON. Yes, we've had a nice chat. Didn't we, Walter . . .

WALTER. Yeah. (DORIS *throws her coat on the couch and turns to her father*)

BOLTON. (*He sees that* DORIS *is very pregnant. He stares for a moment, then manages a jittery smile*)
Is that a . . . baby?

DORIS. (*Nodding happily*) Uh-huh.

BOLTON. When is it, uh—?

DORIS. (*Blithely*) Oh, any time now.

BOLTON. (*He smiles wanly at* WALTER, *who is beaming proudly, and says hopefully to* DORIS) Well, uh, why didn't you tell me before. When you first got married?

DORIS. I did.

BOLTON. You really just got married yesterday?

DORIS. No, no. We've been married since Tuesday.

BOLTON. Since Tuesday . . . (*His hope fades abruptly*) Oh. (*He rouses himself and makes a valiant effort at enthusiasm*) Well, gee, isn't this wonderful! You're going to have a baby! Well, congratulations, Doris! (*He crosses to her and kisses her awkwardly*) Congratulations, uh, Walter! (WALTER *steps in as* BOLTON *crosses to him and shakes his hand*) This is really marvelous! A baby! Isn't this great!

DORIS. (*Not fooled for a minute*) See, I told you we should have waited.

WALTER. No.

BOLTON. Of course you should have waited!

12

DORIS. No, I mean we were going to wait until after the baby was born so that people wouldn't think we got married just because we *had* to.

WALTER. But we were so much in love, we said, "Well, the hell with what anybody says, let's get married!" (DORIS *crosses to* WALTER. *They put their arms around each other*)

BOLTON. Good thinking, Walter! Too bad it didn't occur to you sooner. (*He turns away, giving up the pretense that everything is fine*) Doris, why didn't you tell me before? All those times you talked to me on the phone, and you didn't tell me you were pregnant.

DORIS. I'm sorry, Daddy, but this was something we had to resolve by ourselves. We had to make sure marriage was the right thing for us, that's all.

BOLTON. And you think you can find that out in nine months? Why, sometimes it takes *years* to wreck a marriage! (*He is struck by an appalling thought*) Oh, my God, what will your mother say?! She's going to blame this whole thing on me! I'll never hear the end of it! (*He looks down at his stomach*) Oh, that bitch of an ulcer has just been waiting for something like this to happen. I can see those rows of yogurt containers already! (*He starts to move about aimlessly*)

DORIS. Don't worry, Daddy, I'll tell Mother when the time comes.

BOLTON. When what time comes?

DORIS. When the *right* time comes. Now you just sit down over there and take it easy. I have a wonderful dinner planned. (*Crosses to kitchen area*)

BOLTON. (*Turning slowly*) Well! I can see that this whole thing is just a big lark for you! And why not?! What do your friends around here care how long you've been married; they're probably too stoned to count anyway! But *I* have to go back and tell them in Chicago. *They* can count, and believe me, they *will!*

DORIS. Oh, Daddy, you've never had any respect for those people, why bother with them now?

BOLTON. I *have* to bother with them, I live with them! They're all over me! Oh, boy, your mother's family will just *love* this! There's nothing like a nice juicy piece of gossip to get the social season off to a flying start!

WALTER. (*Having stood this as long as he can*) Now, wait a minute, it's not our fault if you're hung up in Chicago.

BOLTON. (*Indignantly*) *I am not hung up in Chicago!*

WALTER. If you can't enjoy your daughter's child, you're hung up *somewhere!*

BOLTON. Goddammit, I *am* enjoying it! I *am!* . . . It's just

14

that I don't particularly like having a lot of smug jerks snickering behind my back! And I really think it's very inconsiderate of you, Doris, to embarrass your mother and me socially like this.

WALTER. Well, I'm very sorry our child is a cause of social embarrassment to you. I'll speak to him about it. (*Yells at the baby*) Hey, you, did you hear that? You're a cause of social embarrassment! Your grandfather hates you!

BOLTON. (*Shocked*) *I didn't say that!*

WALTER. (*As before*) *He didn't say that!* Well, what did you say, because I got to straighten the kid out. He doesn't know he's supposed to punch in on a social time clock. He might think we don't love him.

BOLTON. (*Still upset at the accusation that he hates the baby*) Look, I have nothing against the *baby*. I'll . . . I'll love him. I love children. It's just that if he were to be born a little later, it would be better for everybody.

WALTER. It wouldn't be better for *him*. You can't wish for a later birth without wishing this child out of existence, and how do you know he won't develop a cure for the atom bomb?

BOLTON. I'd be satisfied if he'd just figure out what to tell them in Chicago! (*He gives up, and sits wearily on the end of the couch, rubbing his stomach*)

WALTER. (*Blandly*) Oh, now, I think we ought to be able to work out something here. Isn't this really just a public relations problem?

BOLTON. (*Sarcastically*) You might call it that, yes.

WALTER. Well, aren't you in advertising or something? You ought to be able to come up with an angle here. I mean, why tell them about the baby at all?

BOLTON. (*Ironically*) Well, they're going to have to know about it sooner or later. I can't just suddenly produce a teenage grandchild! (*Thinks*) Of course, by then, a lot of the relatives will have died off . . .

WALTER. Wait a minute! Now, I'm just talking off the top of my head, you understand, but what's wrong with this? . . . We let a few years go by, and then we announce that we're going to *adopt* a child!

BOLTON. (*Trying to decide how to take this*) Well . . .

WALTER. (*Quickly*) Good, I'm glad you like that. We'll stick the kid in an orphanage until then, which will put us way ahead, costwise, and really get them in the ole pump when the great day arrives! You'll be there, with, say, Raymond Burr at your side—we get the medium two-shot through the orphanage gate—cut to a close-up of the little, tear-streaked face . . . *Gram-pa!*

16

(BOLTON *has risen and moved upstage of couch, his face frozen with the realization that he has been taken for a ride*)

DORIS. (*Concerned, she crosses to* WALTER *and says quietly to him*) Go down and get a container of yogurt. (WALTER *crosses to the door and turns*)

WALTER. What flavor?

BOLTON. (*Flatly*) Plain.

(WALTER *exits. After a moment of silence,* BOLTON *turns to* DORIS)

DORIS. Shame on you, Daddy!

BOLTON. I don't want to put the kid in an orphanage, for God's sake! I only hesitated there because I was polishing up a devastating comeback.

DORIS. That's what I mean, you were being deliberately rude. I'm sure you've hurt Walter's feelings. He's very sensitive.

BOLTON. Yes, I can see that. He reminds me of myself when I was young. I used to wear my sister's necklace, but I finally gave it up when I learned to walk.

DORIS. What's the matter with you? I've never seen you like this!

17

BOLTON. (*Indicating her condition*) Well, I've never seen you like this! My God, how could this happen to a girl with your background?

DORIS. (*Evenly*) Just lucky, I guess . . . What *is* this anyway?! You're coming on like the squarest father alive!

(*During the following scene, she busily moves around between the kitchen and the table, setting the table and preparing dinner.* BOLTON *hovers awkwardly about, feeling rather like a stranger*)

Really, Daddy, I'd hate to have Walter get the wrong impression about you; he has a tendency to be a little skeptical about advertising men anyway.

BOLTON. I detected that.

DORIS. Most of the ones he knows *have* sold out and he's having a terrible time himself trying to live truthfully. I'm sure you can help him.

BOLTON. (*Uncomfortably*) Oh, well, that's a very personal thing, Doris, I don't think I could help him with that.

DORIS. Why?! You've always helped me!

BOLTON. Yes, but you're my daughter.

DORIS. (*Gaily*) Well, now you've gained a son.

18

BOLTON. Yeah. I have to tell you, Doris, there's something about him that gets on my nerves. I don't quite know what it is . . .

DORIS. Oh, that's silly, Daddy. You and Walter are really very much alike—except that he's twenty years younger.

BOLTON. That's what gets on my nerves! Oh hell, it's not just him. Lately, I've had the feeling that your whole generation *knows something* I don't know.

DORIS. (*Tying on her apron, says on an impulse, indicating her baby*) *This* is my generation.

BOLTON. What do you mean?

DORIS. (*Lightly*) Well, generation originally meant giving birth and all . . . so this is *my* generation, and I'm *your* generation. Did you know *that?*

BOLTON. No, but that's *not* the kind of thing I'm talking about!

DORIS. It always upsets you men because you can't give birth.

BOLTON. Not me! I don't want any part of it!

DORIS. (*Setting the table, she rattles on cheerfully*) Ah, but way down deep you *do!* Why, in some of these primitive tribes I've been reading about, the husband stages a symbolic delivery at the same time his wife is in labor. He acts out the labor and all, with the relatives making a big fuss over *him*. And the real mother is giving birth all by herself out in the *bushes*, and then she brings the baby in and gives it to her husband, and he pretends he delivered it himself!

BOLTON. (*Fascinated in spite of himself*) Is that right?

DORIS. Oh yes.

BOLTON. Hmm. Well, at least it gives him something to do.

DORIS. (*Pauses, and says quietly*) Yes, that *is* important, isn't it? What I was going to say before is that Walter takes the baby very seriously. When I first told him about it, he reacted . . . as if I had conferred some great honor on him, and . . . well, I'm very happy with Walter, Daddy.

BOLTON. Yeah, well, I definitely don't think he should yell at the baby like that, he's going to make it a nervous wreck!

DORIS. (*Teasing*) Didn't you ever talk to me like that?

BOLTON. Certainly not! Well, maybe I said, "Hello in there" or something like that, but I never *yelled*.

DORIS. (*Stops, faces him*) Aren't you *glad* I'm so happy?

BOLTON. Of course I am, sweetheart. (*They embrace*) Oh, Doris, I miss you. I don't have anybody to talk to. You're the only one who knows what I'm really like.

DORIS. (*Gently breaking away*) How *is* Mother?

BOLTON. (*Morosely*) Oh, just the same. Mad all the time.

DORIS. At what? Me still?

BOLTON. No, me mostly. She's decided I'm drinking too much.

DORIS. Are you?

BOLTON. (*Ruefully*) Yes.

DORIS. (*Looks at him a moment and decides not to comment. Instead she says*) I thought the best way to tell her would be to just give her a darling little baby to hold.

BOLTON. (*Skeptically*) Well, let's hope it looks exactly like her.

DORIS. (*Reassuringly*) Don't worry, Mother and I won't be fighting any more.

BOLTON. (*Almost alarmed*) What's the matter? Why won't you be fighting?

DORIS. Oh, I understand her better now that I'm married too. Anyway, what's there to fight about? I have everything I want now. And when she gets to know Walter . . .

BOLTON. (*Incredulously*) *This* is all you want? (*She nods, smiling*) You mean to tell me that after all those goddam

21

schools, all you want is this terrible old, broken-down, rat-infested . . .

DORIS. We're getting a dog that's practically a Scotty. They're wonderful ratters.

BOLTON. My God, you mean it *is* rat-infested?

DORIS. (*Blithely*) Well, just a little.

BOLTON. Jesus! I don't know. I just do not know . . . Well, I suppose that's just one of the little inconveniences you have to put up with when you marry a beatnik.

DORIS. Walter isn't a beatnik.

BOLTON. Oh no, of course not! Nobody is a beatnik around here. It's just like Germany at the end of the war: nobody was a Nazi. You couldn't find one anywhere. What about his parents?

DORIS. They weren't beatniks either. Or Nazis.

BOLTON. You mean they're both dead?

DORIS. Yes, they were quite a bit older.

BOLTON. Well, at least I won't have to meet them for a while. (DORIS *turns away, distressed*) I'm sorry. I didn't mean to be so grumpy . . . Say, I really love your place here. I want to give you something nice for it as a wedding present. How about a new set of furniture? That would help some.

DORIS. (*Getting glasses from the cupboard*) You're kidding! Walter just finished making this! He made all these things himself! I love them!

BOLTON. Oh, I didn't really notice them. Nice wood. He made these? He's a carpenter too, huh?

DORIS. (*Crossing to the table with three glasses*) Oh, he can do almost anything like that. Practically everything we have is handmade. Walter hates anything machine-made. See these glasses? A friend of ours made them. (*Puts two down, hands one to* BOLTON)

BOLTON. (*Eying the irregularly shaped glass dubiously, takes it*) Yeah, they look uh, handmade all right. Very nice. Very honest-looking. Very— (DORIS *crosses back to counter while* BOLTON *puts the glass down on the table, but he can't get it to stand upright and is afraid to let go of it. Finally he says*) I can't get this glass to stand up.

DORIS. (*Looking, says matter-of-factly*) Oh yes, well that one you have to lean against something. (*He leans it against something on the table*) It's all right when it's half full.

BOLTON. Say, listen, how about if I just give you money, and you buy whatever you want. (DORIS *hesitates again*) Now don't tell me he prints his own money! (DORIS *laughs, but doesn't indicate acceptance*) What's the matter? You must need money!

DORIS. We don't need money. Walter does very well. He has a nice little photographic business going. I'll show you some of his work after dinner.

BOLTON. I'm not offering to *support* you, it's just a little gift. (*Picks up the glass*) How about half a glass of fifties? You'll need it for the baby.

DORIS. (*Crossing upstage*) I have practically everything I need. I do! (*She pulls a cradle out from upstage of the refrigerator*) See the cradle; isn't it darling! Walter made it!

BOLTON. (*In unison with her*) Walter made it. I know. What's the matter with you? (DORIS *puts cradle away*) Why can't I give you anything? (DORIS *comes back down to the counter and continues making the salad*) You can't be *that* contented! What *is* this?

DORIS. What is what? Relax, will you?! I just wish you'd hold off for a while, that's all. Please, Daddy. Let's talk about something else.

BOLTON. (*With an effort at brightness*) Well, uh, what does the doctor say about the baby? (*She stops working for a beat.*) What's the matter?! My God, there's nothing wrong is there?!

24

DORIS. No! No. Everything is normal. Will you please relax! No wonder your ulcer's back!

BOLTON. Doris, if there's something wrong with the baby, tell me.

DORIS. Daddy, there is nothing wrong! Look, Daddy, please, this is my first dinner for you and Walter together, and I wish you would just try to think calm thoughts or something. Please. He's really a wonderful person, let's all have a nice dinner together. It means a lot to me.

BOLTON. Sure, baby, sure. I'll be ole Genial Jim, King of the Backslappers. Of course, he hates that . . .

(*The door opens.* WALTER *enters*)

WALTER. (*Exuberantly holding up a bag*) Hey, Doris, guess what! I ran into Bullets Farnsworth and she paid me for that enlargement of her girl friend! So I bought wine for dinner! (*He produces a half-gallon jug and starts filling the glasses on the table*)

DORIS. Wonderful! Oh, how lucky! . . . (*She helps* WALTER *fill the glasses*) Can you drink it, Daddy?

BOLTON. Well, so long as business is booming . . .

WALTER. Great! This is a very fine wine . . . (*Displays the label*) See! The label was copyrighted in 1959, an excellent

25

year! You see it in all the best doorways around here. (*He and* DORIS *laugh*)

BOLTON. (*Eying the wine dubiously*) I'll drink a toast to the baby, anyway. (*They all get set for the toast.* BOLTON *raises his glass*) Well, to the Little Stranger . . . (*Then to* WALTER) . . . and to the Big Stranger . . . (*Then to* DORIS) . . . and to the . . . Sudden Stranger. (*He drinks deeply*)

(DORIS *and* WALTER *look at each other and then drink. There is a moment of awkward silence and* BOLTON *says*)

Well, I'd better get ready for dinner; where's the bathroom? You do have one, don't you? (*He laughs, they do not*)

DORIS. (*Rousing herself*) Oh, sure, Daddy. (*She points upstage to the door above the kitchen*) Right in through here, on the left there . . .

BOLTON. Handmade, I suppose . . . (*He exits*)

(DORIS, *disturbed, turns back to the kitchen*)

WALTER. (*Grimly*) I've already made my mind up. I'm not going to tell him.

DORIS. Please, Walter, give him a chance.

WALTER. I did. You saw how he reacted to your being pregnant. He's a phony liberal. He's really hostile as hell.

26

DORIS. You've had him on the pan ever since he got here.

WALTER. What do you mean? He's had me in the electric chair, practically! Listen, he's the kind who'd have the cops after us if he found out we were going to deliver the baby ourselves.

DORIS. (*Anxiously*) No, he isn't, Walter, he'll want to help us. I'm almost sure he will . . . he's been so good to me all my life, I feel that I owe him a chance to be part of this.

WALTER. Now, Doris, you agreed that *I* would decide whether to tell him or not.

DORIS. (*Pleading*) All I'm asking is that you not make your mind up right away. Talk to him a little more, get to know him a little better. Don't jump to conclusions, he says lots of things he doesn't really mean.

WALTER. All right, but it's very dangerous, Doris. Once he knows, he *knows*.

DORIS. (*Submissively*) All right, Walter, I'll leave it up to you, but can't we have a nice dinner anyway? Please?

WALTER. Sure. I bought wine, didn't I?

DORIS. Yes, sweetheart, that was very good of you. Thank you. (*Kisses* WALTER's *cheek*) Uh, maybe it would help if you took the necklace off.

WALTER. I said I was going to wear it today, and that means *all* day.

DORIS. Yes, but it's after sunset, the day is technically over.

WALTER. (*Tempted*) Hmm . . . I hate to take advantage of a legal loophole . . .

DORIS. Come on, darling, I'd like to wear it for dinner.

WALTER. (*Removing it*) Oh, all right, the damn catch pinches my neck anyway. (*He puts it over her head*)

DORIS. It pinches mine too.

WALTER. (*Starting to remove it*) Why didn't you tell me! I'll fix it!

DORIS. (*Holding his hands*) No. They're like little love nips.

WALTER. Depraved creature! (*They kiss*)

DORIS. (*Breaking from* WALTER *and guiding him down toward where he has left his jacket*) It would be so nice if you'd wear your jacket for dinner. (*She gives him another little kiss*)

WALTER. There you go, controlling me with sex again. (*He crosses down and puts on the jacket*) I can just see the headline in the *Village Voice*: "Love Slave Sells Out—Dons Jacket."

(As WALTER *buttons his jacket and straightens his tie,* BOL-
TON *emerges from the upstage door with his jacket in his
hand, crosses to desk, and hangs his jacket on desk chair*)

BOLTON. I thought I'd get comfortable for dinner.

DORIS. Very sensible, Daddy. Oh, Walter, why don't you get
comfortable too?

WALTER. "Love Slave Sells Out—Doffs Jacket."

(As WALTER *removes his jacket,* BOLTON *notices that* DORIS
now has the necklace.)

BOLTON. Well, what happened to the primitive warrior?

WALTER. (*Turning instantly to* DORIS, *he reaches for the necklace*) Gimme that back!

DORIS. (*Slapping* WALTER's *hand away*) No! Now stop it!
Both of you! Behave yourselves! (*There is a moment of
truculent silence*) Walter, show Daddy your studio.

WALTER. (*Gesturing vaguely upstage*) Uh, this is my studio.

DORIS. (*Takes* WALTER's *jacket from him and gives him a
nudge, saying*) Daddy, you used to be very interested in
photography. He has a wonderful camera.

BOLTON. Well, yes, that was some time ago, of course.

29

WALTER. (*Making an effort*) Well, uh, that's interesting. What kind of a camera do you have? (DORIS *hangs up* WALTER's *coat and gets a camera out of a cabinet*)

BOLTON. Oh, it's a, uh . . . the name escapes me at the moment . . . it's a . . . what *is* the name of that damn thing . . . well, it's, uh black . . . sort of a candid-type camera.

(WALTER *turns away with a hopeless gesture*)

DORIS. (*Returning with the camera, which has a small strobe light attached to it*) This is Walter's favorite camera. It has a little . . . (FLASH) Oops!

(*She has accidentally fired the strobe.* WALTER *takes the camera from her*)

Did I do something?

WALTER. No, it's all right.

DORIS. (*Gaily*) Do me a favor, will you, darling, and take some pictures of Daddy?

BOLTON. (*Appalled at the thought*) Oh, uh, I uh, I don't think . . .

DORIS. Please, Daddy, I want to have some pictures of you.

BOLTON. Why?

DORIS. Why?! Because I'd like to have them. Come on, Daddy, be a good sport.

BOLTON. (*Unable to think of a valid objection*) Well, where do you want me to stand? Back here? (*He moves up into the studio area.* DORIS *crosses to kitchen and starts yogurt dip*)

WALTER. (*Sitting on a stool down at the table*) No, uh, I don't like posed pictures. Just, uh, you know, be normal, and if I happen to see a good picture, I'll just . . . (*He turns quickly and aiming the camera at* BOLTON, *flashes the strobe*) . . . take it.

BOLTON. (*Awkwardly standing up in the studio area, tries to smile as the picture is flashed, but too late. He asks anxiously*) Was that a picture?!

WALTER. (*Enigmatically*) No.

BOLTON. (*Crossing down*) You'll, uh, *tell* me when you're going to take a picture?

WALTER. No, that'd spoil it. Just act normally. Forget about the camera.

BOLTON. (*Feeling acutely self-conscious, starts to sit on the couch, but seeing the camera aimed at him, he stops half-*

way and straightens up awkwardly) Well, uh, I see what you mean about space . . . I noticed you have quite a dark-room out back there.

WALTER. (*Looking through the camera*) Uh-huh . . .

BOLTON. (*Moving upstage*) You use this part for a studio, huh?

WALTER. Yeah, but I don't do much studio work.

BOLTON. (*Forgetting himself, he speaks normally but rather didactically, finger raised*) That's where the money is, you know. (FLASH. *He freezes, staring at his raised finger*) Was that a picture?

WALTER. (*Enigmatically, as before*) No.

BOLTON. (*Crossing down to the table*) Oh. Uh, in terms of business, isn't there a limit to how much you can enlarge Bullets' girl friend? (*He laughs jovially, and picks up his wine glass*)

WALTER. I sometimes do darkroom work for other photographers.

BOLTON. Oh, I see . . . (*He starts to take a sip of his wine. FLASH. He freezes, mouth open to drink, then slowly puts the glass down on the table*) Look, I'm really not in the mood for taking pictures, I'm uh, well, I'm too hungry, actually.

WALTER. Doris, your father is hungry.

DORIS. (*Arranging some potato chips around a bowl of dip on a tray*) I have the yogurt dip right here! (*She hands the tray to* WALTER *who places it in front of* BOLTON)

WALTER. Here.

BOLTON. Thank you.

(*He digs a chip into the dip and starts to raise it to his mouth; as he does so,* WALTER *raises the camera.* BOLTON *sees him out of the corner of his eye and lowers the loaded chip.* WALTER *lowers the camera at the same time.* DORIS *crosses to the table.* BOLTON *starts to raise the potato chip again,* WALTER *keeps pace with the camera.* BOLTON *stops and angrily lowers the chip*)

DORIS. (*Seeing him do this, says innocently*) What's the matter, Daddy, don't you like the dip?

BOLTON. He's trying to catch me eating it!

DORIS. (*Pleased*) Oh, your first bite in our house!

(*Taking advantage of this distraction,* BOLTON *jams the chip into his mouth, turning away from* WALTER *as he does so.* WALTER *doesn't attempt the shot*)

BOLTON. (*Angrily to* DORIS, *his mouth full*) Will you please make him stop that!?

33

DORIS. Stop what?

(*His mouth still full,* BOLTON *turns and points angrily at* WALTER, *who instantly snaps his picture, as he does so.* FLASH)

BOLTON. That!

DORIS. Daddy, you don't realize what a good photographer Walter *is!* Darling, show Daddy your book.

WALTER. (*Puts camera on table*) Oh, he wouldn't want to see that . . .

DORIS. (*Crossing down right to get the book*) Oh you're such a lox about your own work!

BOLTON. Oh, do you have a book in progress?

WALTER. Doesn't everybody?

DORIS. (*Showing a bulky loose-leaf notebook*) Here, Daddy . . . See, it's photographs, and poetry . . .

WALTER. (*Crossing down right, where he moves about in anxiety during the reading of his verse*) It's not poetry, it's just light verse.

BOLTON. (*Reading the title*) "Eleven Kinds of Petulant Whines"! Yours or other peoples?

34

WALTER. Both.

DORIS. (*Reading*)

All the mating cries are shrill,
In this our summer fester-ville
Of Love . . .
For we are the sallow men, tinted with Tanfastic,
For we are the callow men, bristling with bombastic,
For we are the marshmallow men, peter bog soldiers,
Drastic . . .

(BOLTON *looks up, baffled*)

Isn't that a riot! He has another funny one about impotence in here too . . . (BOLTON *reacts. She is looking through the book, and comes across another*) Oh, wait! Here's another one of my favorites . . . we made a song out of this. Sing it, Walter.

WALTER. What? "Impo-tenting Tonight"?

DORIS. No, "Pianola."

WALTER. Oh, Dorrie . . .

DORIS. All right then, I'll sing it. Will you do the "yeah-yeahs"?

WALTER. (*Reluctantly*) All right.

35

(DORIS *hums to get on pitch, and then launches into the following in an old Al Jolson piano-roll style, with a touch of rock and roll*)

> I put my IBM card in that ole pianola,
> And it played out my whole life song!
> I never knew-ew-ew-ew I was a rock and roller,
> Till that melody came along!

WALTER. (*Sings*) Yeah, yeah, yeah!

DORIS.

> My Rorschach was swinging,
> My Percentile was hip.
> My Conformity Index just made me flip.
> When I put my IBM card in that ole pianola,
> And it played out my whole life,
> It played out my whole life,
> It played out my whole life song!

DORIS *and* WALTER. (*In unison*) Yeah, yeah-yeah, yeah!

BOLTON. (*Amused and pleased*) Hey! That's very, uh, catchy! (*He laughs and returns to the book*) You took all these pictures, huh?

WALTER. Uh-huh.

BOLTON. They're surprisingly good. (DORIS *looks significantly at* WALTER)

WALTER. (*In response to her prodding*) Thank you.

DORIS. (*Crossing to kitchen, says to her father*) See! I told you!

(*During the following, she continues to prepare dinner*)

BOLTON. (*Still looking at the book*) Yes, indeed, *very* good. I may not know the name of my own camera, but I know a good photograph when I see it. I've been dealing with them for years. Uh, Walter, I uh, I don't suppose you'd want to go into advertising photography.

WALTER. God, no!

BOLTON. (*Quickly*) Yeah, well, that's what I figured. You're right of course. The only reason I mentioned it at all is that I do have all these friends who could get you started.

WALTER. Oh yeah, I'm sure you must have lots of contacts.

BOLTON. Well, these are more than contacts, these are friends who owe me favors for one thing or another. I've saved them up and I can only collect them once, but if you were at all interested, I'd be glad to give them all to you as, well, as a kind of dowry or something . . .

DORIS. (*Melting*) Oh, Daddy . . .

WALTER. (*Rises*) Well, that's very nice of you, but I have to go my own way.

BOLTON. Of course you do, and I'm sure that one of these days, you'll actually get started. I really didn't expect you to go against your beatnik religion, but I had to make certain because there is so much money involved. I mean, with my help you could gross over a hundred thousand the first year. Not that I think you should compromise your principles just to give Doris and the baby a better life. (*Rises, glass in hand*)

WALTER. (*Crosses to the table and picks up his camera*) Yes, well, I'm glad you're not like those guys who try to get other people to sell out so they won't feel so bad about their *own* sellout.

BOLTON. Yes, and I'm glad your attitude is so *refreshingly different* from that stupid beatnik stereotype.

DORIS. Oh, Daddy, Walter saw through that whole beat thing years before we had even *heard* about it.

(WALTER *takes* DORIS' *picture as she briefly assumes a comic pose, then he turns and aims the camera at* BOLTON)

BOLTON. Yes, but has he seen through himself yet? (*Defiantly holding the glass up to his mouth*)

38

WALTER. (*Lowers the camera*) Do you believe in the Golden Rule?

BOLTON. Uh, yes.

WALTER. Well, I don't want to do ads unto others because I *hate it* when others do ads unto me. (WALTER *crosses up to the cabinet and puts the camera away*)

BOLTON. Very well put, Walter. That's very biblical of you. Uh, do we have time for another glass of wine?

DORIS. Sure, Daddy.

BOLTON. (*Pouring himself some more wine*) What makes you think you can continue indefinitely as a teenage drop out?

WALTER. I'll admit I've taken a long time to find myself. I had to find Doris first. (DORIS, *moved by this, crosses to his side*)

BOLTON. Well, now that you have her—for better or for worse —it's high time you started making it better.

DORIS. I'm not sure I could stand making it *much* better. (WALTER *and* DORIS *kiss*)

BOLTON. Well, I don't blame you for being afraid to try commercial photography. You'd have to compete with some fantastic photographers. They can do this kind of stuff with their feet.

WALTER. (*Crossing to* BOLTON, *he picks up his book*) But do they *do* it? I mean have you personally ever seen any of these guys' pictures like this . . . (*Shows* BOLTON *a picture*)

BOLTON. (*Glancing at the picture*) When a man is flying all over the place making two or three hundred thousand a year, he doesn't have time to hang around waiting for some neurotic tuba player to throw up.

WALTER. (*Crossing down right to put book away*) Well, I'm relieved to hear that. I wouldn't want any of those guys moving in on *my* racket.

DORIS. Daddy, do you know anyone who could help Walter get his book published?

BOLTON. No. (*He and* WALTER *pace up and down, trying not to fight. Suddenly* BOLTON *blurts*) We ad men are holding this whole economy together! What do you think of that?

WALTER. (*Mildly*) I think you're probably right.

BOLTON. (*Angrily*) Don't be patronizing.

WALTER. I didn't say I liked it!

BOLTON. Well, I didn't say I liked it either, did I?!

DORIS. (*Brightly*) See, I knew you two were in agreement all along.

WALTER. Yeah, except that *he does* it!

BOLTON. No, I don't, I don't do any of that hard sell stuff any more. I've been moving more into the area of public relations. I have mainly institutional accounts. My things are informative, dignified . . . Here, I'll show you, I have a little pamphlet right here. (*Crosses to coat on chair and gets pamphlet, comes back and shows it to* WALTER) It's for welcoming and orienting new employees. See, history of the company, portraits of the company officials, brief biographies . . . Say, maybe you'd be interested in taking some of these portraits . . .

WALTER. (*Spotting something in the pamphlet*) Did you write this? This right here?

BOLTON. (*Looking*) Uh, yes.

WALTER. My God, you're a public relations genius! (*He reads to* DORIS) ". . . so strong was his devotion to the Company that he didn't have a single absence in the thirty-two years from the day of his employment as stock boy to the day of his self-defenestration as president!!" Self-defenestration!

DORIS. What does it mean?

WALTER. It means that after thirty-two years of perfect attendance, he threw himself out the window.

41

DORIS. Daddy! To dispose of a man's life with a phrase like *that!*

BOLTON. Well, I probably shouldn't have mentioned it at all, but it was in all the papers and, well, what the hell could I do? As a matter of fact, this was considered very clever handling of the problem. All right, so it's fudging a little. These things happen. You have to live with them.

WALTER. (*Upset, he crosses to down right, throwing the pamphlet on the table as he passes it*) You have to, we don't.

BOLTON. (*Losing control of himself*) You're not living, that's why! You're afraid to! You're afraid to get out and take your chances with the rest of us, so you hide down here in your rat-infested ivory tower, and take potshots at everybody else! It's easy, it's fun, and it's *very safe!*

DORIS. Daddy! Stop it! What do you want from him?

WALTER. (*Calmly*) He wants respect.

BOLTON. (*This hits him hard. He stares for a moment, then covers angrily*) Respect! *Don't make me laugh!* You can't afford to show *anyone* any respect! (*He turns and walks upstage*)

DORIS. Please don't be hurt, Daddy.

WALTER. Well, I'll be glad to *show* you respect, but *true* respect is involuntary.

42

BOLTON. (*Turning around, a note of appeal in his voice*) But you don't *know* me! I'm a very liberal-minded man! Aren't I, Doris?

DORIS. Sure you are, Daddy, and you're a *nice* man.

BOLTON. And I'm a *nice* man. All right, so I happened to go into advertising. I'd like to have gone back to school after the war under the GI Bill and become a doctor or something, but I had family responsibilities and they came first!

WALTER. (*Deliberately casual*) You considered becoming a doctor?

BOLTON. Yes. A buddy of mine wanted me to go to medical school with him. (*Turns to* DORIS *with a sudden thought*) Say, he's an obstetrician. Maybe you should call him. Who do you have now?

WALTER. (*Cutting in quickly*) Yeah, you should have been a doctor. It's practically the same racket you're in now, public relations. They have a wonderful setup, you know: they've got all these viruses working for them day and night and they keep the supply of doctors down, see, so there are plenty of viruses to go around. Now, they may not know them all by name, but, I mean, who wouldn't have status with a deal like that? They're *it*, man, the supreme authorities from the cradle to the grave. Why, the very instant a child is born today, it falls right into their hands.

43

DORIS. (*Warningly*) Walter!

(WALTER *catches himself*)

BOLTON. (*To* WALTER) I would *love* to hear you make one positive, constructive statement of any kind . . .

WALTER. (*Airily*) Oh, I'm very positive, and I foresee a very constructive future when the doctors take over the whole country. I wrote a thing about it: about this Doctor-Dictator who's in this patriotic religious procession making his traditional annual house call, in this papier-mâché horse and buggy, with the fake snow blowing on him, and he's going along, blessing the crowd with LSD 25. Oh, you'd love this Doctor-Dictator, he's very positive.

BOLTON. (*Indignantly*) I happen to be for socialized medicine!

WALTER. Oh, beautiful! Throw out *their* rotten institution and stick in *your* rotten institution—they're all the same crooked bureaucrats hiding behind you public relations guys! Name me one institution that isn't rotten! Go ahead! Name one!

BOLTON. (*After a moment of desperately trying to think of one*) Uh—what about the postal service?

WALTER. Ah, you don't give a damn about them! You just like their slogan— (*Places his hand over his heart and recites mockingly*) "Neither snow, nor rain, nor heat, nor

44

gloom of night stays these couriers from the swift completion of their appointed rounds" . . .

BOLTON. (*Turns on* DORIS *and shouts angrily*) You've married an anarchist, you know that, don't you?!

DORIS. (*Rushing to serve the dinner, she says distractedly*) I know, Daddy, but can't we have a nice dinner anyway.

BOLTON. (*Turning back to* WALTER) Goddammit, if you don't believe in anything, what's the idea of marrying my daughter and starting a family?!

WALTER. (*Passionately*) Because that's the only thing I'm sure of! It's obvious we're supposed to pair off like this, a man and a woman, that's the way we're *made*! And that's why I distrust any group bigger than two! We're not made *that* way!

BOLTON. The point is, you two are already three. And—

WALTER. (*Interrupting angrily*) Ah, you know as well as I do that the whole setup is rotten, you just don't have the guts to admit it!

BOLTON. (*Furious*) I have a damn sight more guts than you have! I'm in there fighting to improve it!

WALTER. With what? "Self-defenestration?" Actually, that's just what we need, a new national holiday, Self-Defenestration Day! Clean out the System! (*Jumps*) Ah-h-h-h-h-h-h!

45

DORIS. (*Crossing to table with salad*) Walter, will you toss the salad? Everything else is ready!

(WALTER *crosses to the table and angrily tosses and serves the salad during the following*)

BOLTON. Oh, this town is just full of you smart-asses tearing things down, throwing everything out, good, bad, what's the difference to you? Daddy will fix it. And we will. I don't care what you say, I know the *real* men are with *me*—building, repairing, trying to make things better!

WALTER. If you were, if you really were, I'd respect you. But you're not. You're a hypocrite!

BOLTON. (*Livid*) How dare . . .

WALTER. (*Interrupting*) You claim you're for socialized medicine and stuff like that, and yet you cheat on your income tax which pays for it! You're such a cheat, you can't even come down to see your own daughter without pulling something cute! (*To* DORIS) You know what he wrote down in his expense book for the trip down here? *Taxi to Photographers!*

DORIS. (*Shocked*) Daddy! You didn't!

BOLTON. Oh, for God's sake, everybody does that!

DORIS. (*Takes the empty salad bowl and puts it on the*

46

counter) Daddy, you take the money for our wedding present and you pay your taxes with it.

WALTER. What wedding present?

(BOLTON *paces around above the couch*)

DORIS. Don't get upset, there won't be any. (DORIS *crosses and puts her apron away*, WALTER *paces down left*)

BOLTON. All right, so I won't deduct it! I'll take my dirty advertising money and give it to the tax collector! *He'll* take it! Will that make you happy?!

DORIS. (*Crosses to table*) You have to be honest for yourself, Daddy. Being honest for other people doesn't count. All right, everybody sit down! (*She sits up center*, WALTER *paces up and down stage left as* BOLTON *paces stage right*)

BOLTON. This is ridiculous! Doris, you can't reject me, your own father, just because I deducted a taxi fare!

DORIS. We're not rejecting you, just your money.

WALTER. (*Sitting on the left stool*) Ignore us financially.

BOLTON. How can I ignore you financially, you're part of my family! (*He has a sudden insight*) You *know* I can't ignore you. You *know* I'll keep after you until I force you into the System! And then you can enjoy being rich without feeling

47

guilty! You married my daughter so you'd be *forced* into the System!

WALTER. (*Passionately*) I will not be forced into the System under any circumstances!

BOLTON. You're in it already! You couldn't *exist* without the System, the Water, the Gas, the Police Department, even the doctors! Your child will fall into their hands like everybody else's!

WALTER. (*Losing control of himself*) No, it won't! Because I'm delivering it right here *myself!* (*He catches himself*) Oh dammit, I told him!

DORIS. Oh, don't worry, darling, he won't say anything.

BOLTON. (*Incredulously*) Won't say anything!

DORIS. (*Rises*) If you do anything to spoil this, Daddy, I'll never speak to you again! *I mean that!*

BOLTON. Do you actually expect me to stand by and let you do an insane thing like that!

(WALTER *rises*)

DORIS. (*Still trying to keep it light*) No, don't stand by—boil water!

BOLTON. You're kidding me.

48

DORIS. (*Dropping all effort at pleasantness, says sternly*) I'm not! Daddy, if you won't help I want you to at least promise me you won't interfere. Promise me or I want you to leave right now!

BOLTON. How can I promise a thing like that!

DORIS. (*Resolutely*) Get his bag.

(WALTER *starts to cross up*)

BOLTON. (*Seeing she means it, he capitulates*) All right . . . I promise.

(WALTER *comes back*)

DORIS. (*Embracing her father*) Oh, I knew you'd come through! (*She sits happily*) Now, let's all have a nice dinner.

(DOLTON *sits slowly, as*)

THE CURTAIN FALLS

ACT II

At rise: JIM BOLTON *is alone on stage. His coat is draped over the desk chair and he is wearing a different shirt. The afternoon sun again slants through the large plate-glass windows.* BOLTON *has one of them pivoted open.*

BOLTON. (*Leaning out and calling down*) Stan! Up here, Stan! (*He withdraws, runs to the front door muttering*) Why the hell did he have to park right out in front! (*He opens the door and calls tensely down the stair well*) Up here, Stan. (*He turns back into the room and crosses to the right of table*)

(STAN HERMAN *enters. He is about the same age as* BOLTON, *but cheerful, laconic, and relaxed. He wears a handsome gray-herringbone tweed suit*)

STAN. (*Fondly*) Jim! How are ya, Buddy!

BOLTON. Why did you come down here in the big Caddy, and with MD plates?

STAN. (*Taken aback*) It's my *car.*

BOLTON. But I told you, I don't want anyone to know you're a doctor!

STAN. I thought you were kidding! I have to drive a big Caddy with MD plates; what do you think all that Latin on a doctor's diploma says?

BOLTON. You old dogface, you haven't changed a bit!

STAN. You have, you look terrible. (*Sits on a stool*)

BOLTON. Thanks, I feel terrible. I still have a headache from that cheap wine. I don't know how those winos can stand it. Of course, *they* get to sleep it off in the gutter. *I* lay awake all night worrying about Doris and listening for those goddam rats.

STAN. Did you hear any?

BOLTON. I don't know, I don't know what they sound like.

STAN. Where is Doris?

BOLTON. (*Pacing angrily about*) They've gone to a hootenanny over in the Village. He's an amateur folk singer . . . (*Indicates studio*) and an amateur photographer . . . (*Indicates furniture*) *and* an amateur carpenter . . . (*Indicates book of poems*) *and* an amateur poet . . . *and* an amateur necklace maker, and *wearer*, I might add! However he is a *professional* Puritan! He's some kind of goddam beatnik Honor Scout!

STAN. (*Still concerned about* JIM's *health, he rises and points to a vein in his temple*) Take it easy, Jim, your, uh, what-dayacallit vein there is pulsing like a bastard.

BOLTON. Boy, you've really built up an impressive medical vocabulary!

STAN. I'm not trying to impress you, I'm trying to keep you from having a stroke.

BOLTON. Yeah, well, it would serve her right if I did. If I ever thought she'd marry somebody like . . .

STAN. (*Interrupting in surprise*) You mean they're married?

BOLTON. Certainly they're married!

STAN. Well, all you said was that Doris was pregnant. You sounded so upset, I assumed . . .

BOLTON. No, no! Listen, I have a right to be upset! Just wait till you hear this, you won't even believe it! Get this now. You ready? The baby is due any day now, and, they have no doctor, and this guy she married is planning to deliver the baby *himself* right here!

STAN. No kidding?! (*He seems more intrigued than alarmed*)

BOLTON. Can you *imagine!* Now I ask you, what kind of lunatic would want to deliver his own baby?! Or *any* baby for that matter! I mean, my God! It's insane! It's . . . (*He*

notices STAN *has turned away with a quizzical expression*)
What's the matter?

STAN. Well, nothing, except that my life's work is delivering babies.

BOLTON. Yes, but you're an *obstetrician!*

STAN. Well, before I was an obstetrician, I was just a kid who wanted to deliver babies. When they take that first breath, Jim, it's a tremendous thrill. I feel it every time.

BOLTON. But this is a completely different situation here! This is an appalling situation! I'm amazed that . . . !

STAN. Jim! Don't get so excited. I don't think a home delivery is a good idea at all. It could be very dangerous. I think you should definitely try to talk them out of it.

BOLTON. (*Turning away in mock chagrin*) *Oh, I wish I'd thought of that!* (*Turning back, normal*) They wouldn't even let me get started. Doris kept threatening to cut me out of her life and she has just enough of her mother in her to hold a grudge indefinitely. And *now!*— Who knows what she'll do? She's lost all touch with reality! My God, she just got married last Tuesday! *That's* how much she knows what she's doing.

STAN. Well, when you're in love and nine months pregnant, that isn't *too* dumb, you know.

BOLTON. It was just a whim! They happened to be passing City Hall or something.

STAN. Jim, you always said you were going to bring Doris up to be a free, independent woman—so you did such a good job, she's independent of you too.

BOLTON. (*Pacing in agitation*) There's a difference between being free and being *crazy!* Anyway, she's *not* free, this guy dominates her completely! She's kissing him every five seconds! I tell you, Stan, it's enough to give you an Oedipus complex! (STAN *can't help laughing*) Yeah, you're some consolation, you are. I couldn't wait for you to get down here to tell you about this, and all you've done so far is laugh at me and criticize my veins! Meanwhile, my daughter's life is at stake!

STAN. I'm sorry, Jim, I don't mean to take the situation lightly, but there's no need to panic yet, is there?

BOLTON. Who knows? They don't know when it's due, they've never been to a doctor! They don't even know if everything is all right! I mean, I've been playing along with them just to gain time, but I've got to act fast!

STAN. What do you mean, you've been playing along with them?

BOLTON. Well, uh, Doris made me promise not to interfere.

54

STAN. (*Concerned*) You promised her you wouldn't interfere?!

BOLTON. I *had* to!

STAN. (*Regarding him for a moment, then says lightly*) Did you cross your fingers, or anything?

BOLTON. (*Distressed*) No, I didn't think of it. Listen, they were going to throw me right out! What could I have done then?

STAN. Well, what are you going to do now?

BOLTON. Well, first I want to show you this terrible place they're planning to deliver the baby in. (*Crosses to show* STAN *the room.* STAN *follows*) He's built this especially for the baby. Look at this! (*He knocks on the partition next to the door. It sounds very flimsy*) It's the only delivery room in New York made out of second-hand plywood.

STAN. (*Having entered the room, looks around briefly, then emerges, his face grave*) They're really serious about this, aren't they?

BOLTON. What the hell have I been telling you?! Listen, I think we should sneak over to the hootenanny and try to spot Doris. I mean, maybe she should have a Caesarean or something—that would solve everything.

STAN. What am I supposed to do, examine her during a dosey-do?

BOLTON. (*Embarrassed*) Well, I thought maybe you could, you know, bump into her or something.

STAN. Jim, there's more to it than that, *believe it or not!* I have to examine her in my office, with the nurse and everything.

BOLTON. Oh, he'd never let her go!

STAN. Can't you get her alone somehow?

BOLTON. No, they're always together, thick as thieves! This guy is a fanatic. So is she for that matter. (*Crosses to desk, opens it and sits*) Here, look at all these medical books they have! These are not to be believed! They showed me these last night—and I went into shock on the first picture! (*He hands* STAN *two books*)

STAN. (*Taking a book*) Hey, they're going to try the Lamaze Method?

BOLTON. I don't know, some wild thing. She's been exercising and *breathing* for weeks, apparently.

STAN. This isn't wild. It works. Concentration on the breathing suppresses the pain. Some of my patients have delivered by this technique without any medication at all. I'm all for it.

BOLTON. If Doris was your patient, I'd be all for it too. It's this do-it-yourself maniac I'm worried about. Look, he's had his nose in this one all morning. (*Hands* STAN *a book*) This book has some of the most God-awful pictures I have ever seen!

STAN. (*Greeting the book as an old friend*) *DeLee's Obstetrics!* Boy, this takes me back!

BOLTON. I *thought* it looked old! Completely out of date, I suppose.

STAN. Well, not really; the actual birth process hasn't changed much lately.

BOLTON. (*Looking in another book*) Well, it's high time they did something about it! (*He winces at a picture*) Ooh! He *deliberately* leaves these around here in his desk for me to look at!

STAN. (*Reading a piece of paper being used as a bookmark*) Say, does this boy seem unusually depressed or anything?

BOLTON. (*Rises*) No . . . why?

STAN. Well, he has a rather odd note scribbled on here . . . "Said the president to his VP, I'll push you and you push me, on that Great Self-Defenestration Day."

BOLTON. Oh, that son of a . . . (*He snatches the paper from* STAN) Oh, yeah, uh, don't pay any attention to that. It's probably just some silly poem he's working on. He has a whole book of that junk. Here, look at this, it will give you some idea of what I'm up against here! (*He gives* STAN *the book of poems, and as* STAN *sits down to read it he circles around, thinking*) Say, uh, Stan, they made a crack about my boiling water, and, uh, I mean, you always hear that, and I was just wondering if you could tell me what they use that for—*without going into too much detail!*

STAN. Washing.

BOLTON. Well, uh, washing what?

STAN. Everything. The cleaner everything is, the less chance for infection.

BOLTON. That's all it's used for?!

STAN. Well, you could make yourself some instant coffee with it.

BOLTON. Some instant gin would be what *I'd* need! They don't have a thing to drink here. Sunday, all the liquor stores closed . . . I don't know . . .

STAN. Let's go out to a bar and unlimber your expense account.

BOLTON. Yeah, they called me on that, too.

STAN. On what? Drinking?

BOLTON. (*In an embarrassed tone*) No, cheating on my income tax. I tell you, Stan, it's been like a nightmare.

STAN. Come on, let's go. We'll use our own money.

BOLTON. No, now that I think of it, I'd better wait here for this lawyer to call me back.

STAN. What lawyer?

BOLTON. Oh, a young fellow from the agency here. Used to date Doris in Chicago. I should never have helped him get transferred here to New York. If he had stayed in Chicago, she might have married him instead of this character assassin.

STAN. (*Concerned*) Why bring a lawyer into this?

BOLTON. (*Pointedly*) Well, it's becoming more and more apparent from your attitude that I'll be forced to take legal action here. Do you think I'm going to let this guy walk all over me, endangering my daughter's life?! I'm going to slap him down with some kind of injunction or something! (*Crosses up to window, looks out down the street*)

STAN. (*Becoming even more concerned*) Look, Jim, if you really want me to go over to the hootenanny, I'll go. I'll probably get arrested for trying to molest her, but let's go.

BOLTON. (*Coming back down*) No, you're right. It's foolish. This requires action! I'm not going to evade my responsibility as a father. I'll move so fast he won't know what hit him! Damned anarchist! He's not satisfied with marrying my daughter, he's got to kill her too!

STAN. That doesn't sound like you, Jim. Did you have some kind of terrible fight with this boy, something personal?

BOLTON. No! I didn't mind arguing with him.

STAN. About what?

BOLTON. Everything! Advertising, politics . . .

STAN. You argued about advertising?! How?! You mean he's *for* it?

BOLTON. No, he *hates* it!

STAN. Well, so do you, don't you?

BOLTON. Sure, but he won't grant me that! He doesn't believe I'm trying to improve things from within!

STAN. (*Understanding*) Oh. Are you?

60

BOLTON. Certainly! It's just that, uh, well, you know how it is . . . (STAN *smiles*) Yeah? Well, that the hell are *you* doing about your whole damn rotten medical system?!

STAN. (*Airily*) I happen to belong to a highly secret group of eminent specialists known as the Knights of the Red Crayon. During medical conventions, we write subversive slogans on the walls of the men's room. Like "Vive la Medicaire!" or "Surgeons, cut carefully—the fee you split may be your own!"

BOLTON. Oh, that's childish for crying out loud! If you feel like that, why don't you liberal guys get together and break up that damn lobby!

STAN. Oh, come on, Jim, that's Forties thinking.

BOLTON. (*Appalled*) *Forties* thinking! You mean the nineteen forties?!

STAN. Sure, you've heard of the Thirties, haven't you? The Forties came next—twenty-five years ago.

BOLTON. God! (*Pause*) Are you in on their secret?

STAN. What secret? Who?

BOLTON. These young kids. I have the feeling they all know something I don't know.

61

STAN. The only one of their secrets I know is that they use Saran Wrap for a contraceptive.

BOLTON. Isn't that awful! Does it work?

STAN. How do you think *I* get to know about it? These young kids keep me up-to-date though. That's how I can sort of dig your friend here.

BOLTON. Well, he won't dig you. He hates doctors, and you're just a part of System-serving, Big-money medicine.

STAN. What if I borrow somebody's Volkswagen?

BOLTON. Forget it, Stan, you'll never be up-to-date enough for this guy.

STAN. Oh, I don't know: he's not so far out. Hating advertising happens to be fifties thinking. The fashionable attitude today is amused contempt. What you're really supposed to hate now is the Telephone Company. Actually, this boy sounds like a nice, old-fashioned kid. Why don't you like him?

BOLTON. I wish to hell you'd stop trying to be funny about this! Anyway, you're wrong. He's very big with the amused contempt. I offered him the opportunity of a lifetime; I offered to use my influence to set him up as a commercial photographer, and he laughed at me and spit in my face, practically. How's *that* for amused contempt!

STAN. (*Finally understanding*) Oh. And you're not sure he's wrong.

BOLTON. Oh, my God, another *Reader's Digest* psychoanalyst!

STAN. Well, I have to get it for my waiting room. What does Doris say about all this?

BOLTON. Oh, Doris! Her main concern at the moment is that I may contaminate the place with a wedding present! Well, she'll see: *I'll* have the last laugh when the baby gets bitten by a rat!

STAN. Ycah, that'll be a riot!

BOLTON. (*Flustered*) What I mean is . . .

STAN. (*Interrupting*) Oh, Jim, Jim, you don't know *what* you mean, you're so mixed up! They've got you on the ropes, Buddy, and . . .

BOLTON. (*Interrupting*) Well, dammit, I came down here in a liberal-minded way, completely ready to accept this guy into my own family, and what happens? They won't let *me* into *their* family!

STAN. I know you're hurt, Jim, but try to cool it a little. If you start throwing your weight around, you'll be blamed for *anything* that goes wrong here.

63

BOLTON. Yes, and if I don't interfere I'll be blamed for letting it *happen!* And if I *help* them even, anything that goes wrong will be traced to my defective boiled water! My God, all I'm trying to do is to keep my daughter from dying in childbirth.

STAN. Are you sure that's all you're trying to do? Are you sure you're not also using this to put that boy down?

BOLTON. That's a helluva thing to say! All I want is for Doris to have that baby safely!

STAN. But don't you see, Jim, that's not all *she* wants. She wants a beautiful experience as well, which is what most young women have come to expect from childbirth these days. Times have changed, Jim.

BOLTON. (*Crossing suddenly to the medical book and opening it*) But childbirth hasn't! What if she gets a prolapsed cord? He's got it marked here in red!

STAN. (*Taken aback somewhat*) Well, they might lose the baby, but she'd probably be all right.

BOLTON. (*Very upset*) But I don't *want* them to lose the baby!

STAN. I said they might!

BOLTON. What about hemorrhaging? How would she get a transfusion in time?! That's marked here too.

64

Act I. WALTER: "Dorrie! Your father's here!"

Act I. BOLTON: "Will you please make him stop that!?"

Act II. STAN: "Well, to law and order, and like that."

Act II. DORIS: "Please, Daddy, don't make me choose between you and Walter!"

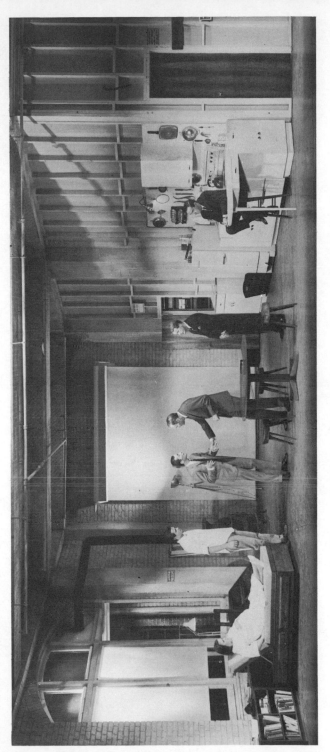

Act III. KEN: "Well, I don't pretend to be a poetry expert either, Jim."

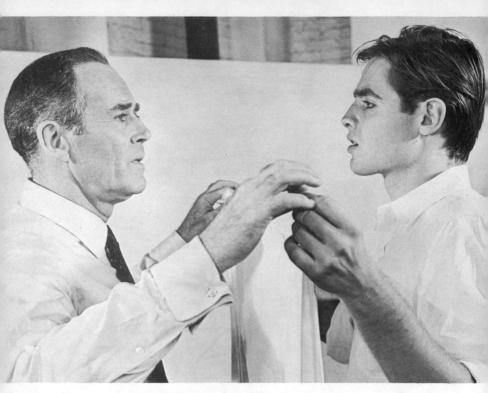

Act III. WALTER: "Thanks."

STAN. Well, that would be bad. But statistically, she's got a better chance of getting hit by a car coming back from the hootenanny.

BOLTON. That'll probably happen too. Another beautiful experience!

STAN. Jim, all I'm saying is that we have to consider Doris's state of mind.

BOLTON. I'll tell you what we have to consider: Is it or is it not more dangerous, much more dangerous, for him to try to deliver her here than for you to deliver her in the hospital? Yes or no?

STAN. Of course it's more dangerous, but . . .

BOLTON. *Much* more dangerous . . .

STAN. (*After a pause, says reluctantly*) *Much* more dangerous . . .

BOLTON. (*Pressing hard*) She could die right there in that room, couldn't she?

STAN. (*Quietly*) Yes.

BOLTON. Then why are you for it?

65

STAN. (*Uncomfortably*) I'm not, Jim, I'm not! But this baby is probably the most important event of her life so far, and now that I see how completely committed they are, I realize that if you lose control of yourself, and mess things up, she will never forgive you. I know you told me that before, but you don't really believe it. Well, you'd better believe it —pregnant young women, I know about—*she will never forgive you!*

(BOLTON *stares at him. The doorbell rings*)

BOLTON. That must be the doorbell . . . (*He picks up* WALTER'S *book and the medical books, crosses to desk, and puts medical books away. The doorbell rings again. He quickly closes desk and crosses back, putting* WALTER'S *book on the counter, and as he crosses to the door, says*) Try not to look like a doctor.

(STAN *is stumped by this request but finally, he removes the pens and thermometer from his breast pocket and turns the lapels and collar of his jacket on the inside, making it look like one of those lapel-less, hipster jackets*)

BOLTON. (*Calls down the stairs*) Who is it?

WINN. (*Offstage*) It's Winston Garand!

BOLTON. (*Offstage*) Winn! I didn't mean for you to come way down here on a Sunday afternoon! I thought we'd just do this on the phone.

(WINSTON GARAND *enters followed by* BOLTON. WINN *crosses to right of table. He is pleasant in appearance, and has a warm, well-modulated voice. He is extremely polite, almost self-effacing, and he has a very nice smile. He wears a dark blue blazer, gray slacks, and carries an attaché case*)

WINN. Well, sir, as an old friend of the family, I thought it the least I could do under the circumstances,

(*As* WINN *enters,* STAN, *trying to be as hip as possible, starts to dance the frug.* WINN *turns back to* BOLTON, *sees* STAN *and trails off*) and it *is* rather complicated . . .

(BOLTON *turns, sees* STAN, *and stares.* STAN *stops frugging, smiles sheepishly*)

BOLTON. What the hell is the matter with you?

STAN. (*Feeling foolish, says with irritation*) I thought you wanted me to disguise myself?!

BOLTON. Not with him! He's on our side . . . fortunately! Winston Garand—Doctor Herman. (*Notices* STAN'S *coat collar*) What happened to your coat?

STAN. (*Turning it back out with difficulty*) I *ruined* it for *you!* That's what happened to it! (*He turns away rather huffily*)

BOLTON. (*Sits*) Sit down, Winn. What were you saying about complications? (WINN *puts attaché case on table*)

67

STAN. (*Off to one side, still trying to get his coat back into shape, disgustedly mimics to himself* BOLTON's *rather querulous tone:*) What happened to your coat?

BOLTON. Ignore him, Winn.

WINN. (*Opening his attaché case*) Well . . . Oh, here, sir, I thought this might come in handy on a Sunday. (*He takes a bottle of good Scotch out of his case.*)

BOLTON. Well! That comes in handy *any* day! That's very thoughtful of you, Winn.

STAN. (*Immediately brightening, crosses and relieves* BOLTON *of the bottle*) Here, I'll make them. We were just discussing this very problem, and you've provided a splendid solution . . . (*Waggles the bottle*) . . . splendid *solution* . . . Get it? (*He gives* WINN *a broad "traveling salesman" wink*)

WINN. Oh yes. Heh, heh, very good, heh, heh. (*To* BOLTON *as he sits*) I never met a funny doctor before.

BOLTON. (*Sarcastically*) Oh, he's a card!

STAN. (*Working on the drinks*) Yep, that's me—just a card in the computer of fate. Do not fold, spindle, or mutilate—although I have the feeling I've been spindled somewhere along the line.

BOLTON. (*Acidly*) If *Doctor Boffo* will shut up for a minute, I'd like to hear what you've found out!

68

WINN. (*Pleasantly friendly*) Well, I'm afraid, sir, that your legal position is somewhat ambiguous, because, as far as the law is concerned, you're not an interested party . . .

BOLTON. Not inter—?!

WINN. (*Continuing smoothly*) That's a legal term, sir. It means that you can't request court action on your own behalf, because the law does not consider that *your* rights are being infringed in this situation.

BOLTON. You mean to tell me that a father doesn't have any right to protect his own daughter?

WINN. Yes, but she has to be a minor or *want* to be protected and as I understand it, in this case . . .

BOLTON. But she doesn't know what she's doing!

WINN. Well, since she is over twenty-one, and in full possession of her faculties, the law assumes that she *does* know what she's doing.

BOLTON. And that *I'm* an idiot!

WINN. I'm sure the law doesn't mean anything personal, sir.

STAN. (*Crosses with the drinks*) Here you are, gents, drink up. Well, to law and order, and like that. (*Drinks*)

BOLTON. Wait a minute! Winn, let me get this straight.

STAN. (*Loudly*) Court's adjourned!

BOLTON. Wait a minute! Winn, let me see those notes . . .
(*He tries to set down his glass, but it won't stand up*) I
would get this one! (*He drinks down half the glass, explaining to* WINN) It's all right when it's half full. (*It still won't
stand up*) I must have gone past it . . . (*He takes* WINN's
*glass and starts to pour a little into his, and then suddenly
realizing the idiocy of what he's doing, exclaims:*) Oh, what
the hell am I doing? (*He gets up angrily*) Where'd you find
these glasses, Stan?

STAN. Over there, but there aren't any others.

BOLTON. (*Seething with frustration*) I don't know, I do not
know! (*He leans his glass against something on the counter
and turns back to* WINN) There must be some way I can
stop this. Can't I get this guy for practicing medicine without a license? He doesn't really know what he's doing; Doris
could die right in that room there!

(*During the following,* STAN *crosses to the counter and pulls
out the stool, sits and starts leafing through* WALTER's *book
of poems*)

WINN. I know, sir, but that would be difficult to establish particularly before the fact, and even then childbearing is a
natural condition, not a disease, and if he performed no

70

surgery and administered no drugs, but merely assisted his wife in natural childbirth, it might not even be considered practicing medicine, and furthermore, there are certain religious groups that . . .

BOLTON. (*Throwing up his hands*) All right! *All right!* I don't know what the hell he's always bellyaching about the system for, it's all on his side! (*Rises*) A father doesn't stand a chance these days. They've taken everything away from us: dignity, authority, respect—everything except the responsibilities! . . . Where'd I lean my glass? (STAN *hands him the glass. He drinks.*)

WINN. Well, if I may continue, sir, there are other ways of getting your injunction.

BOLTON. Oh? (WINN *glances questioningly at* STAN) Oh, that's all right, Stan is one of my oldest friends.

WINN. (*Smiling pleasantly at* STAN, *he rises and crosses to him*) No offense intended, Doctor, and, of course, it would come under the heading of a professional confidence, anyway.

STAN. Of course. (*He matches* WINN's *smile tooth for tooth*)

WINN. (*Turning to* BOLTON, *pleasantly matter-of-fact*) Well, as you may recall, sir, the agency handled several political campaigns last election, and some of the bills have not been paid, except, as in the case of one judge, by certain favors.

Therefore, I made a discreet inquiry, and determined that he would also favor you in this matter.

BOLTON. (*Frowning*) What do you mean?

WINN. Well, sir, this judge would take the unborn child under the protective custody of the court.

BOLTON. (*Rather appalled*) Can he do that?

WINN. Oh, certainly, sir, when a child is considered to be endangered by the actions of the parents, the court often steps in to protect the life of the child. Just as you, yourself, are trying to do. This judge would order Doris into a hospital for a normal delivery.

BOLTON. Oh, Walter would never let her go.

WINN. He wouldn't have any choice, it would be a court order. They'd have to obey it.

BOLTON. I see. Well, of course in that case the baby would be *literally* taken by the System. They'd never forgive me . . . But at least Doris and the baby would be safe.

WINN. Which I assume is your main concern here.

BOLTON. (*Very disturbed*) Yes, of course, it has to be . . . It *has* to be . . . What do you think, Stan?

STAN. (*Who has been reading* WALTER's *book while listening to this, says*) Well, I'll just let the frame-ee speak for himself: (*Reads*)

> The soul of man,
> Despite his pride,
> Is rather odd,
> A toy balloon
> Blown up by God,
> Or, strictly speaking,
> The air inside,
> And *that* is leaking.

(*He raises his glass in a toast as* BOLTON, *upset by the verse, turns away*) To poets and young lovers, wherever you are! I've always been for young lovers anyway, they're good for business. (*Drinks*)

BOLTON. (*Crossing back*) I didn't say I was going to do it, did I? We're just, uh, brainstorming here!

STAN. (*Holding out his hand, palm up, and glancing skyward*) Let me know when it lets up.

WINN. (*Moving in with deceptive casualness*) Doctor, am I to infer from your attitude that you don't think this amateur home delivery would be dangerous?

STAN. (*Uncomfortably*) Well, I er . . .

BOLTON. (*Testily*) He thinks it would be dangerous but *fun!* *I'm* the only one who cares, so, of course, I'm the *heavy!*

73

WINN. I assure you, sir, that I also care. I'm very fond of Doris.

BOLTON. Well, thank you, Winn. Walter's only concerned in screwing the doctors out of a baby. I knew he'd be a lousy father the moment I saw him wearing that necklace.

STAN. (*To* BOLTON) Well, I care too, for God's sake! (*To* WINN) But I also happen to know how much his daughter's love means to him; I care about preserving *that* too!

WINN. I'm afraid, Doctor, that I prefer "Safety First" to "Sentimentality First." To attempt a delivery here without a sterile delivery room, without blood supplies, without antibiotics is absurdly dangerous.

STAN. Well, I could leave Jim a supply of tetracycline or some other oral antibiotic.

WINN. (*Casually*) Well, now, if you're willing to accept responsibility for the medical direction of this case, we'll go along with that.

STAN. (*Rises, says evenly*) I can't take the case until they give it to me.

WINN. (*Returning with some sharpness*) I see, you won't accept responsibility yourself, yet you counsel Mr. Bolton not to fulfill his responsibility. How do you justify your position, Doctor?

STAN. Well, I just think that we should try to use persuasion on the boy before crushing him with legal power. Maybe I

74

can persuade him to let me deliver the baby if I take him into the delivery room with me.

WINN. He wouldn't be impressed with that offer, it's becoming quite common! And when he finds out we know of his plans, they'll just slip off to some hide-out and have the baby under even worse conditions. (*To* BOLTON) I'm afraid, sir, we must strike without warning them.

STAN. Jim, I wish you'd let me try to talk to them first.

BOLTON. (*Having followed their argument with increasing concern*) Well, Winn does have a point about not warning them. I mean, right now, they think I'm going to *help* them. Anyway, Stan, I told you, he *hates* doctors. (*Crosses to the counter*) Look there, if you don't believe me . . . read the one about the Doctor-Dictator making the annual house call. (*Finds it for* STAN) Read that! Just read it!

WINN. Sir, I think we should take immediate advantage of this judge's offer.

BOLTON. Easy, Winn. There's no need to panic yet, is there?

WINN. Well, sir, I feel that you should reach a decision and act before they return, because we do have a time problem here. This judge will not be available tomorrow or Tuesday.

BOLTON. Oh . . . (*He looks to* STAN *for help*)

STAN. (*Finishing the poem*) You're right, he *does* hate doctors.

BOLTON. Yeah . . .

WINN. What we need right now is some physical evidence of their intent to deliver their own child. (*He starts looking around the room*)

BOLTON. I haven't decided to do that yet!

WINN. I know, sir, but if you should, we would have to move immediately. What physical preparations have they made for the delivery?

BOLTON. (*Crosses to delivery room*) Well, he's built this whole little room here. It's all very nice and clean. They're going to use it for a nursery later.

WINN. We need something *portable*, sir, something you can take into court when you swear out the warrant. (*Crosses right, looking*)

BOLTON. Oh. (*He stops by the table, caressing the wood*) He made all this furniture himself. Everything they have is handmade.

WINN. (*Crosses toward the desk*) That's not against the law, sir.

76

BOLTON. (*Ruefully*) Well, it won't be long before it will be.

(*The phone rings. They freeze.* BOLTON *crosses to it and picks it up gingerly*)

Hello? . . . Oh . . . (*He turns to* STAN *in amazement*) It's for you!

STAN. (*Crossing to phone*) Probably my service.

BOLTON. (*Puts down phone and crosses away, saying critically*) What if she had called and Walter or Doris answered?

STAN. When I gave her this number, I didn't know we'd be under martial law. (WINN *crosses up right to examine the bookshelf.* STAN *picks up the phone*) Hello? . . . Yeah . . . all right, I'll leave shortly. . . . Who? . . . All right, I'll call them. (*He breaks the connection and dials, saying as an afterthought*) All right to use the phone?

BOLTON. (*Absently*) Sure.

(*He has been watching with increasing concern as* WINN, *still on the prowl, drifts down and goes into the delivery room*)

STAN. (*Into phone*) This is Dr. Herman, what's the trouble, John? . . . No, you're right that's not good. Better put her on . . . (BOLTON's *attention is diverted from* WINN. *He lis-*

77

tens as STAN's *voice becomes very authoritative*) Eleanor, you *know* you can't have any chocolate glop in your skim milk! . . . I don't care *what* it's fortified with, you'll get a big fat behind like you did the last time! . . . Well, I can't help being mean, that's what my middle initial, M, stands for: Stanley Meanie Herman . . . Okay see you Tuesday, 'by. (*He hangs up and crosses back to the counter*)

BOLTON. You needed eight years of medical school for *that?!*

STAN. (*Takes his drink*) Certainly, that's what makes you mean.

WINN. (*Emerges from the delivery room and crosses down right of table and puts a stethoscope on it*) The only medical instrument I could find is this stethoscope, which isn't very incriminating . . .

BOLTON. (*With a slight touch of paternal pride*) They're going to use *natural* childbirth. The Lamaze Method. No drugs or anything.

WINN. (*Getting an idea*) Maybe we could borrow some instruments from Dr. Herman here?

STAN. (*Thinking fast, says evenly*) All mine are monogrammed.

BOLTON. (*Shocked*) I couldn't do that, anyway.

78

(WINN, *unperturbed, crosses down right, and looks through the books next to the couch*)

STAN. (*Closing* WALTER's *book*) It's a shame he's backed himself into such a tight corner on this doctor business. It would be a tremendous loss of face for him to accept any obstetrician who hasn't at least lost his license by treating junkies for free, or something.

BOLTON. Yeah, him and his damn face! He's more of a hypocrite than I am! If that book was ever published and well received, he'd fall all to pieces! He'd kiss the System's feet!

STAN. Then get it published.

BOLTON. I might just do that! . . . as a matter of fact, that's not such a bad idea. You know, that's a standard technique for crushing rebels—make them rich. Now who do I know that . . .

WINN. (*Who has been listening intently while examining the books*) It would take months to get that published, sir.

BOLTON. Yes, but he's hungry for respect, too, and if we could get some editor to give him the genius treatment—you know: fantastic praise, advance royalties—he could afford to lose a little face on this doctor thing. Then we could sell him on accepting Stan.

WINN. When is the baby due, sir? (*He approaches* WALTER's *desk*)

79

BOLTON. (*Lying*) Stan says we have time. (*Crosses up into the studio area, thinking hard*)

STAN. (*On the spot*) Uh, well, probably, yes. For example, Sonia Hallahan, one of my patients, is ten days overdue now—and I wish she wasn't, because I suddenly feel like getting drunk. (*He eats his ice cube*)

WINN. (*Finding the books in* WALTER's *desk*) Say, here are some medical books. They might do the trick. (*He takes them to the center table*)

BOLTON. (*Suddenly getting an idea*) Cutlass! *Cutlass* Magazine! We buy their center spread!

STAN. I thought *Cutlass* was a girly picture magazine?

BOLTON. Yes, but they have some fine writers in between. (*He crosses to his coat and takes out his little book*) I think I have the advertising manager's home number right here . . . Yes! I'm going to call him right now!

WINN. (*Looking through the medical books says ultra-casually*) Uh, sir, I wouldn't advise getting the agency any more involved than it is now.

BOLTON. Than it is *now?*

WINN. Well, sir, since *you* are involved, the agency is involved, and scandal is so insidious that . . .

BOLTON. Scandal!

WINN. (*As pleasant as ever*) Well, sir, if we don't get Doris into a hospital, we might very well have a serious obstetrical accident on our hands. And we might not be able to get the newspapers to suppress it properly because of its entertainment value—you know, a child conceived out of wedlock, beatniks refusing medical aid until it's too late, prominent Chicago advertising man accomplice before the fact— and the nature of your institutional accounts is such that . . .

BOLTON. (*Who has been grimly dialing the phone during the above speech says tensely*) I *know* the nature of my institutional accounts. (WINN, *defeated, crosses up left to the bookshelf.* BOLTON *becomes professionally jovial, speaking into the phone*) Hello . . . Ozzie? This is Jim Bolton . . . Fine, Oz, how are you, pal? I'm in town and I need some *personal* help . . . No, no, no girls. My, uh, son-in-law, I guess you'd call him, has written a book of some great sort of beatnik poetry with pictures . . . drug on the market, yes . . . (*He starts to press*) well, sometimes your center spread is a drug on the market, too, Oz . . . (WINN *turns sharply back to* BOLTON *but says nothing*) . . . Well, this doesn't *feel* like me either, but I'm in a bad thing here . . . Well, I want to take one of your editors to dinner . . . Who? . . . Have him down here by seven o'clock tonight . . . (WINN *crosses tensely to window*) Tonight, Oz, *tonight!* . . . Oz, Oz, listen to me! . . . The address is 437 Broome Street. Owen . . . *Tonight,* Oz . . . Thanks, fella, 'by. (*He hangs up grimly, stares at* WINN *for a moment, and then, putting the address notebook into his shirt pocket, turns to* STAN) Can you join us, Stan?

STAN. (*Concealing his concern*) I think so. None of my patients will deliver tonight, I don't have theatre tickets.

BOLTON. Wonderful! Now, don't let on that you're a big rich doctor, until they . . .

STAN. (*Enthusiastically*) I could pretend to be an alcoholic or something . . .

BOLTON. No, no! I'll just introduce you as an old army buddy, and at dinner, while this editor is buttering up Walter, you can be chatting with Doris about the dangers of childbirth. Then after they get to like you, I'll just casually mention that you're a, uh . . .

STAN. A junkie obstetrician. Swinging Stan the Delivery Man!

(*They laugh.*)

Listen, Jim, I have to go.

BOLTON. Okay, I'll call you later with the exact time and place! (*His confident manner suddenly vanishes as* STAN *moves toward the door, and he runs over to the window*) Wait! Wait'll I see if the coast is clear! (*He peers cautiously down the street*) Okay, Stan, go ahead! (STAN *crosses to door*)

WINN. (*Crossing down*) Good-by, Doctor, it was a great pleasure meeting you!

STAN. Yeah, well, thanks for the booze.

WINN. Oh that was my pleasure, Doctor!

STAN. Well, you're a *polite* sonofabitch, I'll say that for you. See you later, Jim. (*Exits*)

BOLTON. Don't mind him, Winn, he's a rare bird. Nothing fazes him. In the Hürtgen Forest, he was practically the only medic in our company that didn't have a nervous breakdown.

WINN. Should I make a note of that, sir? It might impress your son-in-law. He was never in combat himself.

BOLTON. No, it's only when you have been that you're impressed with it. Anyway, the Army is very high on his list of rotten institutions. In fact, I haven't been able to come up with an institution yet that he hasn't been able to put down . . . (*Thinks*) Say, how'd you know he hadn't been in combat?

WINN. (*Matter-of-factly*) Well, as part of my research, sir, I looked up his service record, which is excellent, nothing we can use there; and he doesn't have a police record.

BOLTON. (*Chilled*) Well, you certainly went to a lot of trouble, Winn. No wonder we have such a good legal department.

WINN. Oh, it was the least I could do, sir.

BOLTON. I'd hate to be on the other side when you were doing your *most!*

WINN. (*Pleasantly*) I don't think you ever will be, sir.

BOLTON. Oh, well, thank you, . . . I guess.

WINN. Who is Ozzie sending down?

BOLTON. Ken—somebody . . .

WINN. Ken Powell, probably, the fiction editor. Sir, my advice is to make the child a ward of the court. It is by far the safest course of action.

BOLTON. Well, Winn, I'm afraid this is just one of those times when I have to take a chance. I'm going to soften him up with this editor, and then try to sell him on Stan.

WINN. All right, sir. Then why don't we all have dinner at my club.

BOLTON. Oh, that, well, that's very nice of you, but . . . (*He hears singing out in the hallway*)

VOICES of WALTER and DORIS. (*Singing as they come up the stairs*)

> On that Great Self-Defenestration Day,
> On that Great Self-Defenestration Day,
> The wigs are loose, the hides are thumpin'
> The whole Executive Suite is jumpin'
> On that Great Self-Defenestration Day.

(*Over the singing, we hear*)

WINN. Is that them?

BOLTON. (*Running around, setting things in order*) That's them all right . . . He's a folk singer . . . Makes up his own songs . . . That's one of them . . .

(WINN, *observing* BOLTON *curiously, takes his attaché case, crosses up left, and waits*)————

WALTER and DORIS. (*The sound gets steadily louder*)

> On that Great Self-Defenestration Day,
> On that Great Self-Defenestration Day,
> Said the president to his VP
> I'll push you and you push me,
> On that Great Self-Defenestration Day.

(*They open the door and burst into the small entryway, downstage left. They are too intent upon their song to no-*

tice BOLTON *and* WINN *who are upstage out of their line of vision.* DORIS *takes coat off and hangs it on the hook by the door*)

On that Great Self-Defenestration Day,
On that Great Self-Defenestration Day,
We'll all be happy as we can be,
With the System gone, we'll all be free!
On that Great Self-Defenestration Day-e-e-e-ah-a-a-a!

(*At the end of song,* WALTER'S *voice slides into the fading scream of a falling man, as he tilts forward and falls into* DORIS' *arms. They laugh happily*)

BOLTON. (*Enraged, he bursts out as soon as they stop singing.*) Oh, yeah? Well what about the Supreme Court?! They're an institution, aren't they? (*Pointing his finger triumphantly*) You *admire* what they've done for integration! Admit it! Ah-hah! Ah-hah!

WALTER. (*Taken aback*) I'll tell you one thing, if one of *them* ever sells out, you can just forget the whole—

DORIS. (*Crossing, suddenly sees* WINN, *stops, bursts out*) Winn! What are you doing here?! (*She is stunned and not particularly pleased.* WALTER *is even less so*)

WINN. (*Crossing to her, pleasant as ever*) Hello, Doris. Nice to see you again. How have you been?

86

DORIS. (*Trying to match his aplomb*) Fine. And you?

WINN. Fine.

DORIS. Oh, uh, Winn, this is my husband, Walter Owen. Winst—

(*As* WALTER *moves forward to* WINN, BOLTON, *who has been thinking furiously, pounces on him again*)

BOLTON. *And what about UNICEF!?* Hah!

DORIS. Daddy, will you *please . . . !*

BOLTON. (*A final thrust as he turns away*) They've been feeding those Asian kids for *years!*

WINN. (*Stepping forward*) How do you do, Walter! (WALTER *shakes hands briefly*) Congratulations! You have a wonderful girl there!

WALTER. (*Putting his guitar away*) I know it.

DORIS. (*Nervously making small talk*) Well, uh, are you still in the public relations department?

WINN. Uh, yes, I am.

DORIS. Oh, that's nice.

87

WINN. (*With a glance at* BOLTON, *who was startled to hear this*) Well, if you'll excuse me, I was just leaving. It's a great pleasure to see you again, Doris, and to meet you, Walter. (*He picks up his attaché case, and moves toward the door.* DORIS *and* WALTER *nod good-by.* DORIS *sits*)

BOLTON. (*Following* WINN *to the door*) I thought you were in the legal department here?

WINN. (*Turns back*) No, sir, I've been in PR for some time now.

BOLTON. I've never seen your name on their regular roster.

WINN. I don't handle any of the regular accounts.

BOLTON. What is your account?

WINN. The agency itself. (BOLTON *stops dead*) Well, good-by, sir, I'll be back at seven with a limousine. (*He goes out and down the stairs*)

BOLTON. (*Recovering his wits, crosses quickly down to the hallway, and calls down the stairs after* WINN) Oh, Winn, thank you for coming down!

WINN'S VOICE. (*Offstage*) It was my pleasure, sir!

(BOLTON *stays out in the hall.* DORIS *is breathing rhythmically. She stops*)

88

DORIS. I just had another contraction! They're getting stronger.

WALTER. (*Checking his watch, he starts for the delivery room*) Five minutes apart. I'd better start getting ready.

(BOLTON *enters slowly from the hall, absorbed in his thoughts of* WINN)

DORIS. Let's wait for one more, just to be sure this is it. (WALTER *waits*)

BOLTON. (*Who hasn't heard this, says to* DORIS *as he crosses down right*) Have you dated Winn since you've been in New York?

DORIS. Uh-huh. Before I met this hunk. (*Says to* WALTER *with a giggle*) Winn was first on Daddy's eligible suitor list.

BOLTON. (*Half to himself*) Yeah, now he's first on another list I have . . .

WALTER. What was he doing here?

BOLTON. Well, uh, I can't help you get your book published without contacting a few people, can I?

DORIS. Daddy! Who?! Tell us about it!

BOLTON. What, and spoil the surprise?

WALTER. I don't want any help from any organization creep carrying an attaché case on a Sunday afternoon . . .

BOLTON. Oh, come on now, Walter, that's Fifties thinking. The fashionable attitude today is amused contempt.

(WALTER *is somewhat taken aback.* BOLTON *presses his advantage*)

You know, I don't think you realize how old-fashioned you've become—the Village poet with the guitar—hating the System—man, that's *over*.

WALTER. What the hell, am I in some kind of originality contest or something?! I don't care how unfashionable something is if it *feels* right to *me!*

BOLTON. (*Pleasantly*) Well, if you're so big with the instinctive approach, why don't you wait to see what my help *feels* like before you reject it? You can't *feel* in advance, you know.

DORIS. I think he's got you, Walter.

BOLTON. Doris *asked* me to help you.

DORIS. I'd love to see that published.

WALTER. (*Reluctantly*) All right. I'll try it.

DORIS. (*Starting to tell him about the baby*) Uh, Daddy, the reason we came home early from the hootenanny is . . .

BOLTON. (*Still feeling rather triumphant*) Just a minute, Doris, I have another little philosophical point I'd like to make while I'm at it.

WALTER. Don't push your luck.

BOLTON. (*Pleasantly to* WALTER) Now, Walter, you've felt the mating instinct . . . (*Indicating* DORIS) Fine! . . . And you've felt the nesting instinct . . . (*Indicating the apartment*) Fine! . . . but another thing you can't feel in advance is the protect-the-young instinct, otherwise you wouldn't *think* of taking such risks with this primitive delivery here!

WALTER. I'll be doing everything I can to minimize the risk.

BOLTON. Except taking a little taxi ride up to a nice safe hospital.

DORIS. Now, Daddy, you promised!

BOLTON. (*Airily*) It's just a little philosophical point.

WALTER. Look, this is our child, it's already stuck with our genes, and it's going to be stuck with our ideals as well.

BOLTON. If it survives.

DORIS. If it survives.

BOLTON. (*To* DORIS) My God, don't you see how selfish you're being! You have to make sacrifices for your children. Believe me, I made plenty for you!

WALTER. More than you should have, if you're still trying to collect for them.

BOLTON. (*To* WALTER) I'm not! But I'll tell you one thing, if she hadn't been to all those fancy schools, she'd never have been able to appreciate *this* dump!

DORIS. (*Gently*) Oh, Daddy, I know you didn't live your life the way you really wanted to. I feel terrible about it. And that's why I know it would be wrong for Walter and me to make a sacrifice for our child that we can't psychologically afford to make. Because then, the poor child would be in debt to us, innocently, and for something that was supposed to have been a gift of love.

BOLTON. (*After a pause*) And you think you're going to control that love? Listen, in a couple of months, that baby will look up into your eyes and give you that first smile, and you will have *had* it! You'll see! You'll get yours! Both of you!

(DORIS, *very moved, crosses to him and embraces him*)

DORIS. Oh, Daddy . . . (*Her eyes fill with tears*)

BOLTON. (*Rather surprised*) Hey, hey, what's that, a tear? Come on now, this isn't like you . . . Say, listen, my turn to treat tonight! We're all going out to dinner, *and* I think we'll be having a very special guest!

DORIS. Not tonight, Daddy. I'm going to have the baby tonight.

BOLTON. How do you know?

DORIS. I'm in the first stage of labor now.

BOLTON. (*Stunned*) You mean you're actually having the baby?! (DORIS *nods*) My God! You're having the baby now? Right now?!

WALTER. Well, it will be some time yet.

BOLTON. (*Starting to panic*) Come on! We've got to get her to a hospital! (*He starts out, stops*) Wait! I'll call first! (*He moves toward the phone, but* WALTER *blocks his way. He stops*) Now listen! I've had enough of this nonsense!

DORIS. Daddy! (*The sound of her voice turns him around*) You promised you wouldn't spoil this!

BOLTON. (*Without thinking*) Yes, but I didn't mean it!

DORIS. You didn't mean it?!

BOLTON. Well, I . . .

DORIS. But you promised me! I've always believed you, you're my father!

BOLTON. If he won't protect you, I have to! Any way I can!

DORIS. (*Tearfully*) Please, Daddy, don't make me choose between you and Walter!

BOLTON. (*After a long pause*) How am I supposed to boil this water?

DORIS. Oh, Daddy! (*She hugs him joyously*)

WALTER. (*Relaxing for the first time, he crosses down left*) I'll be with you in a minute. I want to get the room ready for Doris first. (*He exits into the delivery room.*)

(DORIS *sits on stool right and starts to have another contraction.* BOLTON *hovers anxiously about, the unguarded telephone drawing him like a magnet. Suddenly he gets an idea, and quickly dials a number during the following*)

BOLTON. Say! we're going to need cigars! I know a guy who can get them wholesale!

(DORIS *is concentrating on her breathing and doesn't hear*)

Hello, this is Jim Bolton, is Stan Herman there? . . . Well, where can I reach him? (*He registers acute dismay*) Well, when you hear from him, tell him that my daughter's baby is on the way, and that, uh, I'll need some of his cigars . . . Yes, I know, I know, but you just tell him that. He knows me, Jim Bolton. Tell him to bring them down here immediately! Yes, bring the cigars!

(WALTER *enters, crosses left of table*)

No, I don't have the wrong number, no! . . . (*He has apparently been hung up on, but with a desperate glance at* WALTER *he continues loudly*) Uh, oh, good! Oh, that's wonderful! I'll do that! (*Hangs up, turns to* DORIS *and* WALTER) Listen, this is wonderful! A terrific break on cigars. But I've got to run right over and pick them up right away! (*He grabs his coat and runs to the door*) Wholesale. Dirt cheap!

(*He is out before they can say anything.* WALTER *turns to* DORIS *and they stare at each other worriedly as*)

THE CURTAIN FALLS

ACT III

At rise: The window shades are pulled down, and the studio is lighted by one of the photo floodlights aimed at the ceiling. Pots of water are boiling on the stove.

DORIS, freshly showered and wrapped in a long, white terry cloth robe, is lying on the couch, completely relaxed, having a contraction. The only sign of this is that she is breathing loudly in a special rhythmic manner, inhaling through her nose and exhaling through lightly closed lips as if blowing a feather in front of her face. WALTER is standing upstage of the couch, timing the contraction. The intensity of her breathing builds slightly and then fades off.

WALTER. (*Checking his watch*) One minute, almost exactly. You're doing fine, darling. (*He crosses to table and begins studying his book on obstetrics. He seems very concerned*)

DORIS. (*Happy and proud*) The breathing really works. As long as I can stay relaxed I know I'll be all right . . . (*Notices WALTER at the book*) What's the matter?

WALTER. (*Covering his concern*) Nothing.

DORIS. What are you reading in that?

96

WALTER. I just want to review some procedure, that's all.

DORIS. You seem worried about something, Walter.

WALTER. I'm not worried, I'm just keyed up, like before an exam or something. You'll have to relax for both of us, okay? (*Crosses to* DORIS *and gives her a reassuring pat*)

DORIS. All right. (*She settles back.* WALTER's *worried look returns and he goes back to studying the book*) Would you see if that disinfectant smell is out of the room yet? I know I could relax better on the bed.

WALTER. (*Puts the book in his desk and crosses to the room*) I guess you might as well move in there now as later. The sooner I can hang up the sheets in here and spray them, the better. (*He opens the door, sniffs*) I don't think it will bother you now.

(*Doorbell rings*)

DORIS. Who could that be? I don't think Daddy would ring.

WALTER. It's probably the cops bringing him home drunk.

DORIS. Walter!

WALTER. Well, he looked to me like a guy who had chickened out and was headed for the nearest bar. (*He opens the front door slightly and calls down*) Yes, who is it?

97

MAN'S VOICE OFF. I'm looking for Jim Bolton, is this the right place?

WALTER. Well, he's not here now, and I don't know when he'll be back.

DORIS. Who is it, Walter? Open the door.

(*Reluctantly* WALTER *shuts door of the delivery room, then opens the front door.* KEN POWELL *comes into view*)

KEN. My name is Ken Powell. I'm supposed to meet Jim Bolton here for dinner.

DORIS. Oh, please come in, Mr. Powell.

(WALTER, *although obviously concerned, steps aside and* KEN *enters, crosses toward* DORIS, *then stops*)

I'm his daughter, Doris Owen . . .

KEN. (*Uncertainly*) Oh, how do you do?

DORIS. And this is my husband, Walter Owen.

KEN. (*Turns to* WALTER) Oh, then *you're* the poet! Well, I'm delighted to meet you! (*He shakes* WALTER's *hand*) Actually, it's you I've come down to meet.

WALTER. Me?!

KEN. Yes. My name is Ken Powell . . . I'm the fiction editor of *Cutlass.*

WALTER. *Cutlass* Magazine?!

KEN. You've heard of us?

WALTER. Oh yes!

KEN. Well, we've heard of *you.*

DORIS. (*Thrilled*) Oh, please sit down, Mr. Powell!

WALTER. (*Warningly*) Uh, Doris . . .

KEN. (*To* DORIS) I'm not intruding?

DORIS. No, no!

(KEN *sits on a stool.* DORIS *continues to* WALTER *as much as to* KEN)

It's so kind of you to come all the way down here to see Walter. And I'm sure Daddy will be back shortly.

KEN. (*To* WALTER) Well, they certainly think highly of your poetry. They say it's way out.

WALTER. (*Pleased*) Oh, it's only light verse, you know . . .

KEN. Well, so long as it's way out . . . We're very hip. (*Looks around*) Nice *pad.*

WALTER. Thank you. (*He sees* DORIS, *behind* KEN, *pointing to the bottle, and shakes his head*)

DORIS. (*In spite of this*) Won't you have a drink, Mr. Powell? If Scotch is all right? (WALTER *angrily gets a glass out*)

KEN. Perfect. Uh, do you have any of your stuff around?

DORIS. (*Reaching over to pick up* WALTER's *book*) Oh, yes, right over here . . .

WALTER. (*Immediately rushing to* DORIS) I'll get it! (*He grabs the book and gives it to* KEN) Uh, yes. Well, here's the, uh, corpus delicti . . . you can look through it while I'm fixing your drink.

KEN. (*Slightly baffled by their behavior*) Oh, uh, yes. Well, fine . . .

WALTER. Yes, fine. Just make yourself at home. (*Turns to* DORIS) Uh, Doris, wouldn't you like to rest in the other room?

DORIS. No, I want to hear what he says.

(*He glares at her, and she pokes her tongue out at him.* WALTER *nervously crosses up to the kitchen, and quickly makes a drink*)

KEN. (*Looking at the book, sees the photos*) Did you shoot these pictures?

WALTER. Yes.

KEN. (*Rising and crossing to* WALTER) They're very good! Maybe we should send some of the *girls* down to you! Heh, heh. (*To* DORIS) No offense meant. Heh, heh.

DORIS. What girls?

WALTER. He means the pin-up models.

DORIS. Oh.

KEN. (*As if explaining something to a child*) *Cutlass* is a magazine for intellectuals who like girls. (WALTER *gives* KEN *the drink.* KEN *takes a drink and puts glass on table. To* WALTER) Don't you subscribe?

WALTER. Well, it's kind of expensive for me . . . (*Hastily*) But I read it. Bullets Farnsworth gets it.

KEN. Bullets. Well, that figures. Heh, heh.

WALTER. Yeah. Heh, heh.

KEN. (*Opening to a poem at random*) Well, let's see . . . "Pitfalls of Youth." That's a good subject! You see most of our readers are young-thinking men, and they look to us for guidance. We have a deep moral responsibility to be up-to-the-minute. (*Reads*) Pitfalls of Youth . . .

If in your youth, you struggle free,
And even once live naturally,
Then later, when you fail to make it,
You won't be cool enough to fake it.

(WALTER *and* DORIS *wait for his verdict*)

That's amusing. Yes, that's amusing . . .

(WALTER *and* DORIS *are thrilled*)

(*The front door flies open and* JIM BOLTON *enters, panting and desperate as if he had been running futilely all over town*)

BOLTON. (*Immediately crossing to* DORIS) Doris! How are you?! What's happening?! Are you all right?

DORIS. (*Reaching up to hug him*) Yes, I'm fine! Oh, Daddy, it was so nice of you to have Mr. Powell come down here!

BOLTON. What? Who?

DORIS. (*Indicating* KEN) Mr. Powell from *Cutlass* Magazine.

BOLTON. Oh! (*Suddenly, he sees* KEN *as a possible salvation and turns on his full professional charm*) Well, hello! I'm Jim Bolton, call me Jim. (*He shakes hands warmly with* KEN)

KEN. How do you do, Jim?

BOLTON. (*Trying to feel out the situation*) You've met Walter?

KEN. Sure.

BOLTON. Good.

WALTER. (*With a degree of pride*) He likes it.

BOLTON. (*Delighted*) Good! (*He decides to give it a try*) Ken, I—may I call you Ken?

KEN. Sure, Jim.

BOLTON. (*Although addressing himself to* KEN, *he's really talking to* WALTER) Thank you. Ken, I can't tell you how glad I am that you've come down here to take advantage of this tremendous publishing opportunity!

KEN. Well, I . . .

BOLTON. As I told Ozzie, I want *Cutlass* to get a crack at Walter here, before he gets so big you won't be able to touch him. I feel a sense of loyalty to *Cutlass*—I suppose because I've been buying your center spread for *months*. Heh. Heh.

KEN. (*Weakly*) Heh, heh. (*He sits down meekly and opens the book*)

BOLTON. (*Notices* KEN's *drink*) Uh, why don't you finish that up, Ken, so I can get you another, then you can get down to work. (KEN *gulps down his drink*) How about this Walter? *Cutlass* Magazine! You see, things aren't so bad after all! You'll be famous overnight! (BOLTON *takes the glass*) Good! Now, you just keep a tight grip on that gold football there, and get ready to run with it. This could be the turning point in your career!

(KEN *returns to the book.* BOLTON *crossing to make him a drink, says to* DORIS)

You're sure you're all right?

(DORIS *nods "yes" emphatically.* BOLTON *turns to* WALTER)

How can she be all right?!

WALTER. Where are the cigars?

BOLTON. What cigars? *Oh*, uh, well, I uh . . . I didn't get them. This guy was, uh, hung up in an emergency. He's uh, going to bring them over later . . . (BOLTON *crosses to get water*) Wholesale! Dirt cheap!

WALTER. Oh, good! That's a big load off my mind!

BOLTON. (*Not knowing quite how to take his attitude, crosses to* WALTER) Did, uh, anyone call here?

WALTER. No.

BOLTON. Oh. (*He crosses to* KEN *with the drink*) Ken, isn't this marvelous stuff?! "Eleven Kinds of Petulant Whines"! See,

"Whine Four, Whine Five." It is so great! My idea is to serialize this, say one whine a month, and then on the twelfth month . . . (*He crosses to* WALTER) A picture biography of Walter here, just to round out the year! How does that strike you, Walter?

WALTER. (*Flattered in spite of himself*) Well . . .

BOLTON. (*Moving into high gear*) Good! Actually, Walter is very photogenic and very versatile. We should have shots of him thinking, uh, writing, uh, singing, and uh, maybe sandpapering the furniture a little . . . Wait a minute! Why not have the picture bio the *first* month as a teaser!? That's *it! That's it!*

(DORIS *and* WALTER *are quite caught up by this. There is a knock on the door*)

WALTER. (*Starts to door*) Now who the hell is that?!

BOLTON. (*Stopping* WALTER *and running to the door*) Well now, Walter, this may just be another old friend I've asked to come down and help out. (*Opens door and slumps in disappointment*) Winn . . .

(WINSTON GARAND *enters*)

KEN. (*Rising*) Winn!

WINN. (*Crosses to* KEN) Ken!

(*They shake hands heartily*)

KEN. I didn't know you were in on this!

BOLTON. (*Moving in quickly*) Oh, Winn is an old friend of the family!

WINN. (*Pointing to the book* KEN *is holding*) How do you like that, Ken?

KEN. He has a fine old Ogden Nash quality. I think I can whip them into shape without too much trouble.

(WINN, *satisfied, moves into the background*)

WALTER. (*To* KEN) What do you mean?

BOLTON. (*Trying to get things rolling again*) Well, we can go into that later, Walter, the main thing now is the picture bio. In *color!* Thinking . . . writing . . .

WALTER. (*Still after* KEN) What do you mean, whip them into shape?

BOLTON. (*Anxiously crossing to* WALTER) Now Walter, let's not . . .

KEN. It's all right, Jim, it's a typical neophyte reaction. Well, you see, Walter, as an editor, I am a bridge—an intellectual bridge—between writer and reader. I have to help the author get his neurosis synchronized with the audience's neuroses so that this magic acceptance thing will happen to his neurotic retail products, as I call them.

BOLTON. Oh, well I wouldn't worry about that, Ken, I'm sure Walter has a well-synchronized neurosis! Heh, heh, right, Walter? Heh, heh.

KEN. Yes, but for example, let's take this word "whine." Now our readers are all pretty rugged guys, you know, like your friend Bullets . . . (BOLTON *looks startled*) And, uh, I don't think they would react well to all this whining, particularly if you say, as you do in your satire of T. S. Eliot, here, "We are the callow men. We are the marshmallow men." I think that "We" business is unfortunate. *You* are the callow men! *You* are the marshmallows! You see what I mean? (*Turns to* BOLTON) It reads better.

BOLTON. (*Forestalling* WALTER's *reply*) Wait a minute, Walter. (*Says diplomatically to* KEN) Uh, Ken, wouldn't that tend to change the meaning somehow?

KEN. (*Rising*) Oh, no, I think it would make the message much more inspiring. I mean, you will admit, Jim, that there is a certain pessimistic note running through here, like this one about not being cool enough to fake it.

BOLTON. Uh, yes, but, uh . . .

KEN. We've *got* to give the readers something a little more inspiring here, like say, "If you can't make it, fake it!" See? Upbeat!

BOLTON. (*Not quite so diplomatic*) Well, now I don't pretend to be a poetry expert, Ken, but *that* does change the meaning.

KEN. (*Defensively*) Well, I don't pretend to be a poetry expert either, Jim! (*Sits*) I told Ozzie that when he called me, but he, uh, you know, told me to get my ass down here anyway!

BOLTON. (*Hastily*) Yes, well, let's not go into that! (WALTER *crosses to* DORIS *who is becoming upset*)

KEN. No, but I'm doing my best to help you out, Jim. However, we still have to maintain certain standards of inspiration.

BOLTON. I realize that, Ken, but . . .

KEN. I'm only trying to handle this thing so it won't blow up in my face! I mean, for example, this one about the doctors would cancel out all the waiting room subscriptions! And besides that, *thousands* of our regular readers are very fond of their pediatricians. I remember my own, Dr. Denton . . . I *think* that was his name . . . well, with great fondness. Actually, if it wasn't for him, I don't think I would ever have *made* it even! He'd drive out to our house in any kind of weather. Of course my father, he would always have some kind of sarcastic remark to make about the money it cost!

BOLTON. (*Desperately*) Yes, well, now Walter, here, has a poem about . . .

KEN. (*Not even hearing* BOLTON, *he jumps up and starts spouting*) God! Here's this *doctor* driving all the way out to our house just to see *me*, and all my father can do is bitch about the cost! I mean, now *there's* a subject for you! There's a *real* story there! A Doctor's Devotion.

BOLTON. (*As if dealing with a madman*) "A Doctor's Devotion"—That's lovely, Ken. Now, I . . .

KEN. The mother's a secret nymphomaniac and she has the hots for this young pediatrician, who is trying to avoid her, but he has to keep coming out to the house because the mother is secretly starving this poor little boy. I mean, she's actually *starving* this poor little kid just because of this doctor! And the doctor is just barely keeping the kid alive with these injections, which hurt like hell! So finally, one day the mother tells the doctor she's not going to call him any more—she's mad, see, because she's just rubbed herself all over him and he hasn't even noticed because he's so worried about this little boy . . . That'd be a great scene for the illustration! You know, with the bathrobe . . .

BOLTON. (*Who clearly has been appalled by the story, makes another desperate effort to shut him up*) Oh, that's swell, Ken! Now, Walter's doctor poem . . .

KEN. (*Overriding him*) Wait! W*ait!* I got it! I got the ending! . . . Just to save the little boy's life, the pediatrician does it to her, and the little boy gets up and sees them, and he takes the hypodermic and injects himself in the wrong place and kills himself!

(BOLTON *finally gives up and sinks down on a stool in despair*)

Now *there's* a story for you! A tough, gutsy yarn like that would sell immediately. Why? Because it's real! That's the kind of thing that's happening constantly with *all* these dames . . . (*Realizing the implications for* DORIS) . . . in the suburbs, that is.

(DORIS *rises with* WALTER's *help and they cross to the delivery room.* BOLTON *watches them helplessly*)

WINN. (*Crossing to* KEN) That's a great story, Ken, great! You should write that up.

KEN. I'd like to, Winn, but I just don't have the time. Someday maybe.

WINN. Say, maybe Walter could write it up for you!

KEN. Sure, Winn, anything I can do to help out! You know that!

WINN. What about it, Walter? It would get you started.

WALTER. (*Pausing at the delivery room door, as* DORIS *goes in, he says blandly*) Well, I'll tell you, all those injections make me nervous; couldn't the kid just shoot himself in the mouth?

KEN. (*Coldly*) It's been done.

WALTER. (*More clearly sarcastic*) Oh, well, see, I don't know anything about the suburbs. (*He exits into the delivery room, closing the door firmly.* BOLTON *rises and crosses to the door, very concerned*)

KEN. (*After a pause*) I don't think he liked my story.

WINN. (*Crossing to* KEN) Oh, I'm sure he liked it, Ken.

KEN. (*Petulantly*) He hated it! He hated it! These writers are all the same: they only like their own stuff—no matter what kind of crap it is! (*He slams down* WALTER's *book, and starts to whine as he crosses down left*) When are we going to eat? I'm *starving!*

BOLTON. (*Remembering*) Oh, yes, well, I'll tell you what: why don't you and Winn go on ahead, and we'll meet you there in a few minutes. (KEN *immediately starts out*)

WINN. (*Following slowly, concerned*) Are you sure everything is all right, sir?

BOLTON. Sure, Winn, they're just getting dressed. You two run along.

WINN. (*Dallying*) Well, actually, sir . . .

KEN. (*At the door, whining*) Are you guys trying to starve me or something?!

BOLTON. Run along, Winn, and start eating. (WINN *goes out with* KEN)

KEN. (*As they exit*) Come on, Winn, I'm actually, you know, *starving!*

(BOLTON *closes the door behind them, numbed by a sense of disaster.* WALTER *sticks his head out of the delivery room door, looks to see if they have gone, and quickly crossing to the stove, takes a pair of rubber surgical gloves out of a package and drops them in a pot of boiling water. He is also carrying four folded sheets which he puts on the couch, down right*)

BOLTON. What's happening?! How's she doing?!

WALTER. She'll be all right—now that *that's* over!

BOLTON. Did he throw her off?

WALTER. No, you did! You almost sucked me in there. Boy, you have to watch yourself every minute!

BOLTON. (*Humbly*) I'm sorry he turned out to be so sick. You were right to reject him. But, uh, I hope that won't give you the idea that you should always reject *everyone* because . . .

WALTER. Listen, don't do me any more favors!

BOLTON. But it's not that *simple!* (WALTER *turns angrily away.* BOLTON *crosses right of table*) Wait! Wait! Let me finish! Please! . . . Sometimes, sometimes you have to, uh . . . (WALTER *turns and picks up clothespins*) not compromise! Not compromise! You have to, uh, use jujitsu on the System. You have to fall back, see, and utilizing the weight of the System against itself, you, uh, *flip* the System, and uh . . . (*Seeing that* WALTER *isn't buying the metaphor, he stops in the middle of a jujitsu movement and trails off, feeling absurd under* WALTER's *glare. He crosses to kitchen and picks up the Scotch, to pour himself a drink*)

WALTER. (*With a trace of compassion in his voice*) Are you going to help us, or are you just going to get drunk?

BOLTON. (*Startled, he freezes, then slowly sets the bottle down without pouring and says shakily:*) What do you want me to do?

WALTER. (*Crossing up with sheet*) Help me hang up these sheets.

BOLTON. (*Crosses to* WALTER) What are these for?

(*They hang the first sheet on the stage-left end of upstage line*)

113

WALTER. I'll use them for sterile drapings around Doris.

BOLTON. They aren't sterile, are they?

WALTER. (*Crosses and gets second sheet*) They will be after you spray them with that disinfectant in that sprayer over there. Both sides.

BOLTON. How soon do you think she'll . . .

(*They hang the second sheet on the stage-right end of up-stage line*)

WALTER. Soon enough so that we have to get with it! I lost a lot of time!

BOLTON. Well, then maybe this is one of those times we should outsmart the System by using a hospital.

WALTER. Listen, if you're going to keep that up, you can just get the hell out of here! (*Crosses to get sprayer*)

BOLTON. (*Following him*) No, it's just that I feel responsible that she got off to such a bad start. I mean, can't you blame me for the whole thing and . . .

WALTER. She's going to be all right! You just spray these sheets and keep an eye on that water, and stay off my back! I'm going to do this *my* way, because this is *my* child, and *my* wife, and *my* house! Remember that! (*Gives* BOLTON

114

*the sprayer and crosses to cabinet, gets glass, and starts to
make sugar water)*

BOLTON. Don't worry, I know what it means to have a wife
and child . . . I just wish you did. (WALTER *whirls around,
glaring)* You're still thinking like a single man . . . (WAL-
TER *crosses to delivery room door) . . .* and if you keep it
up, you may *be* one again.

WALTER. *(Freezes, his hand on the knob. He looks back at
BOLTON and says in a strained voice)* She's going to be all
right!

*(He exits into the room, his face tense with anxiety.
BOLTON, very concerned, takes the sprayer, which is like a
hand-pumped Flit gun, and starts spraying. It is a rather
strong-smelling disinfectant. He removes his coat and hangs
it on a hook upstage of refrigerator and then begins spraying the sheets. There is a knock at the door and he crosses
and opens it. WINSTON GARAND enters)*

BOLTON. Winn . . . !

WINN. *(Crosses up right of table)* Sorry, sir, but I forgot my
hat. *(Looks around)*

BOLTON. You weren't wearing one and you know it.

WINN. Sir, is Doris in labor?

115

BOLTON. (*Crossing tensely to* WINN) Isn't it time you leveled with me, Winn? Exactly what are you up to here?

WINN. (*Smoothly*) Well, sir, this is one of those rare times when my duty to protect the agency, and my personal desire to help you and Doris—*coincide*. So when I noticed that Doris was in labor, I sent Ken home, and came back to see what I could do.

BOLTON. (*Dryly*) You have a great future, Winn.

WINN. Thank you, sir. Shall I go for the police?

BOLTON. *No!* No, that won't be necessary, Winn, things are going normally. My God, I've got to spray these sheets. (WINN *puts his bag on the table as* BOLTON *crosses up and starts spraying the stage-left sheet*) Don't ask me what I'm doing. I know it looks ridiculous, but it might help somehow.

WINN. Is Dr. Herman aware of the emergency?

BOLTON. Yes. I chased him all over town and finally located him in a hospital delivering Mrs. Hallahan's baby. It was awful, I had to wait in a little room with the father. He's a jazz drummer and a very nervous man. His name is Hey-Hey Hallahan. Did you ever hear of him?

WINN. No.

BOLTON. He drums on everything. Hey-Hey, Hey-Hey, I thought I'd go out of my mind.

WINN. When will Dr. Herman be here?

BOLTON. As soon as he can, but Mrs. Hallahan has some complication. When Hey-Hey heard that, he started to go crazy on the lampshade, so I raced back here—just in time for *Ken! God!*

WINN. (*Crosses down right and sits on the end of the couch*) I advised against him, sir.

BOLTON. (*Trying to control his irritation*) I know it! Look, Winn, I'd just as soon Walter didn't come out and find you here, he's rather upset with me as it is.

WINN. Well, I think I should at least wait downstairs to talk to the police and the reporters if anything should go wrong, uh, up here.

BOLTON. All right, but let's hope that isn't necessary, for God's sake! (*He starts spraying desperately*)

WINN. (*Rises and crosses to* BOLTON) Uh, one more thing, sir. In the event that some statement is needed for the press, I wonder if you've thought of a euphemistic way to describe what might happen?

BOLTON. Winn, if anything happens to Doris, I won't care about euphemisms or anything else. (*Goes behind stage-right sheet to spray it*)

117

WINN. I know you won't, sir, that's why *I'm* here. (*Gets notes from his attaché case*) Now, the copy people being off on Sunday, I had to take a crack at it myself, but the only thing I've been able to come up with so far is: "The pregnancy resulted in a negative nativity."

BOLTON. (*Appears between sheets, regards* WINN *for a moment, then says ironically*) Negative nativity . . . small "n," I assume.

WINN. Oh yes, sir.

BOLTON. Well, that's very nice, Winn, very dignified, and it will make a helluva folk song. (*He suddenly sniffs at the air*) Jesus, the rubber gloves are burning! (*He races to the stove, snatches the pot aside, and pours in more water*) The goddam water boiled away! I knew something like this would happen! I'm going to get blamed for this whole thing! (*He examines the gloves*) Well, actually, I think they're still all right. (*He puts the pot back, burning his hands a second time*) I know what I can get them for a wedding present: pot holders! (WALTER *bursts out the door, anxiously sniffing the air.* BOLTON *anticipates his concern*) They're all right! They're all right!

WALTER. (*Seeing* WINN) What's he doing back here?

BOLTON. Well, he forgot his hat and came back for it and . . .

WALTER. (*To* WINN) Get out.

BOLTON. Is there anything you need he can run out and get?

WALTER. Like matches for the cigars?

BOLTON. Like emergency medical supplies!

WALTER. You told him!

BOLTON. We may *need* a lawyer before this night is over! (*This chills* WALTER *somewhat*) How is she?

WALTER. Fine. (*He suddenly whirls and dashes back into the bedroom*)

BOLTON. (*Crosses and listens at the door for a moment*) I don't like the way he said that.

WINN. He *is* rude.

BOLTON. (*Angrily*) I meant about Doris!

WINN. (*Picks up case and starts out*) I'd better wait downstairs.

BOLTON. All right. W*ait!* Help me hang up these last two sheets, he can't object to that . . . I don't think . . . (*They hang up the sheets during the following*)

WINN. Why haven't you prepared Walter for Dr. Herman's intervention?

BOLTON. I've been waiting for the right moment, and judging from his reaction to you, it'll have to be a helluva moment.

WINN. Well, you know, this is his house, and he can throw you and/or Dr. Herman out at any time. So actually your foothold here is very precarious.

BOLTON. (*Standing on couch hanging the sheet with difficulty*) Well, Winn, when your whole life has suddenly turned into an old Buster Keaton movie, what's one more precarious foothold? (*Sees something on the rear sheet*) Oh, there's a spot I missed. (*He jumps down, grabs the sprayer, gets back up on the couch and sprays the spot, saying anxiously*) I know I'm not doing this properly. Why doesn't Stan get here? This should be done by a qualified physician.

WINN. I think you ought to prepare Walter *before* he gets here.

BOLTON. (*Spraying downstage-right sheet*) Stan is my last chance. I want Walter to get to like him as a person before I expose him as a doctor.

WINN. But then how will you explain his presence here?

BOLTON. Out-of-town client looking for thrills?

(WINN *doesn't think this is funny.* BOLTON *crosses down to edge of couch*)

I'm sorry, Winn, I suspect my mind is going . . . Wouldn't it be nice if somebody would come and just take me away . . . (*Gets an idea*) Maybe we should call an ambulance! Have it stand by downstairs!

WINN. (*Making certain he understands*) You mean for Doris?

BOLTON. (*Turns indignantly to* WINN) Certainly for Doris!

WINN. It's an excellent idea, sir. (*He crosses and takes phone book and looks up listing*)

BOLTON. (*Guiltily*) I could tell them not to ring the bell or anything and he'd never know they were there. It's ridiculous not to call it.

(WALTER *starts to come out of the delivery room*)

DORIS. (*Offstage*) Walter!

WALTER. What?

DORIS. (*Offstage*) Come back!

(*He whirls and goes back in.* BOLTON *quickly crosses to their door and listens. He turns away, even more worried*)

WINN. (*Locating the listing*) Here it is. There are several . . . this one has the biggest ad.

BOLTON. (*Guiltily picking up the phone*) I don't suppose you can hear that dial tone.

WINN. No, sir.

BOLTON. This is a very loud phone . . . Let's see now . . . (*He dials. It is an old phone and the dial clicks noisily*) Jesus, this is a loud phone! (*Reading the ad while waiting*) Day or night, oxygen-equipped . . . uniformed attendants . . . but no telephone operator! (*They answer*) Oh, hello . . . do you have an ambulance available right away equipped with oxygen and everything? My daughter is having a baby . . . Good. Well send it to . . .

(WALTER *comes out in time to hear this, and runs at* BOLTON *who promptly hangs up*)

WALTER. (*Furious*) I knew you'd try something like this! (*He gets a book out of the desk*)

BOLTON. I was only going to have it *stand by* down there. They have oxygen and stuff. What harm could it do?

WALTER. (*Crosses back to him*) It's the principle of the thing! My God, can't you understand anything!

BOLTON. But it was a private ambulance! It's like a taxi. (*Rises*) You take taxis. This is just a big, long, taxi . . .

WALTER. She's not going anywhere!

BOLTON. (*Frightened*) What do you mean? What happened?

WALTER. Nothing. Everything is fine! It's going to be all right. And we don't need any ambulances or *ambulance attendants* which is what you're trying to sneak in here, *you cheat!* Get out of here! Get out!

DORIS. (*Calling from the room*) Walter! (*He turns and runs back into the room*)

BOLTON. (*Shakily he crosses to delivery room door and listens*) I don't think he really meant me, but you'd better go . . .

(WINN *picks up his attaché case and prepares to leave*)

He really hates me now . . .

WINN. I'll go out to a phone booth and call the ambulance again.

BOLTON. No. Not yet anyway.

WINN. But, sir, you have just as much right to stick to your principles as he has.

BOLTON. Yes, but it's one thing to stick to your principles and it's something else to believe in them. (*He turns back to door to listen*) She seems to be breathing harder somehow. (BOLTON *crosses and sits on stool left*) You know, she says she feels terrible that I haven't lived my life the way I really wanted to . . .

WINN. Oh? What way is that?

BOLTON. I'm afraid I really wanted it the way it was. I hope I get to tell her that.

(*There is a knock on the door,* BOLTON *opens it.* STAN HER-
MAN *enters. He is carrying a paper bag, and a stack of cigar
boxes tied together with a string*)

STAN. (*Very businesslike*) Here's your cigars, Mr. Bolton. You
owe me forty-six twenty. (*He crosses and puts the cigars on
the table, looks around and sees that* WALTER *isn't there*)
Oh, I thought he might be in here.

BOLTON. (*Takes cigars and puts them on desk above couch*)
No, he's in there.

STAN. (*Crossing to counter and putting paper bag down*)
Well, you still owe me forty-six twenty. How's Doris?

BOLTON. (*Indicating the delivery room*) She's in there,
breathing.

STAN. Well, that's always a good sign.

BOLTON. I thought nobody was going to deliver tonight because you didn't have theatre tickets.

STAN. Well, Jim, medicine is still not an exact science. (*He
starts toward the room*)

WINN. Doctor, wait! He still doesn't know about you!

BOLTON. No! God, don't go in there!

STAN. You haven't said *anything* to him?

BOLTON. How can I? Every time he comes out of there, he starts yelling. He just caught me trying to call an ambulance and raised hell about my trying to sneak them into the act.

STAN. (*Concerned*) Oh.

BOLTON. Why don't you listen at the door, there. You can hear her doing that loud breathing.

STAN. (*Crosses to the door and listens. After a moment he straightens up.* BOLTON *and* WINN *wait anxiously for his report*) I don't hear anything.

BOLTON. (*Crossing to* STAN) Well, she was doing that breathing a minute ago. Don't you have a stethoscope or something? Maybe you can hear her better with that.

STAN. Yeah, I'll try it. (*Feeling rather silly he produces a stethoscope from a pocket in his jacket, and listens at the door.*) You've got a fine girl there, Jim.

BOLTON. A baby girl!

STAN. No, *Doris*. She just told *him* not to worry.

BOLTON. Do you think everything's all right?

STAN. I don't know. It's hard enough to tell through the *abdominal* wall.

BOLTON. What are you going to do?

STAN. What do you want me to do?

BOLTON. I don't know. Wait, I guess.

STAN. Okay. (*He crosses and sits on a stool.* BOLTON, *more or less from force of habit, resumes spraying the downstage-right sheet. He stops when he becomes aware of* STAN *staring curiously at him*)

BOLTON. (*Self-consciously*) I'm spraying a disinfectant on these sheets.

STAN. Oh, good idea.

BOLTON. Really?

STAN. Yes, it gives you something to do.

BOLTON. It kills the germs, doesn't it?

STAN. Yeah, I guess so.

BOLTON. You *guess* so?

STAN. Well, let's say that it definitely makes them very nervous.

BOLTON. (*Angrily resumes spraying*) Well, I'm going to do it anyway! . . . It gives me something to do.

STAN. (*Watching him for a moment, he rises and crosses up to* BOLTON) I can't understand why you haven't said something to him about me. This is really very awkward, Jim.

BOLTON. (*Spraying stage-left sheet*) Well, I've been working up to it! I have to lay the philosophical groundwork first. This guy can only be reached on a very intellectual level.

STAN. I see. You mean, he scares the hell out of you.

BOLTON. He doesn't scare me one bit. He upsets me.

STAN. Why?

BOLTON. (*Testily*) Do you mind if I don't bare my soul this red-hot minute?! Why don't you go stethoscope there?!

STAN. (*Trying to jolly him a bit*) What if he were on the other side with his stethoscope, listening to my stethoscope? (STAN *crosses to the door, and listens. The expression on his face becomes solemn. Apparently he hears something of significance. He listens some more, and then takes off his coat and hangs it up by the door and casually crosses to the stove. He takes some instruments out of the paper bag, and from his pockets and slips them into a pot of boiling water. He sees* JIM *watching him intently, says*) Jim, that is some of the finest boiling water I've ever seen.

BOLTON. (*Worriedly*) What if he comes out and sees that stuff?

STAN. I wouldn't worry about that, Jim.

BOLTON. (*Immediately alarmed*) Why shouldn't I worry about it?

STAN. (*Washing his hands*) Don't you have enough to worry about already?

BOLTON. I can fit it in somewhere. (STAN *remains silent.* BOLTON *becomes more and more anxious*) Well?!

STAN. (*Evasively*) Well what?!

BOLTON. You know what! Your not wanting me to worry about that worries the hell out of me, so you might as well tell me.

STAN. (*Turns to* BOLTON) I didn't want to go into it because you're so squeamish, that's all.

BOLTON. Oh, that's very reassuring! It's so horrible you don't even want to tell me?!

STAN. (*Turns off water and dries his hands by shaking them*) Oh, there's nothing horrible about it. I've delivered a couple of hundred of these breech presentations without any trouble at all.

BOLTON. Breech?! You mean the baby's turned around the wrong way?

STAN. It's not wrong, it's just awkward.

BOLTON. How can you tell from here?

STAN. Something he said. (*Crosses down to the wall*) He's just starting to realize that he's in trouble. (*Listens again with the stethoscope in his ears so that he can't hear* BOLTON's *desperate whispers. Referring to* WALTER) He's quite a guy.

BOLTON. You'd better go in there.

STAN. (*Removing the stethoscope*) What?

BOLTON. You'd better go in there!

STAN. (*Crosses to* BOLTON) Jim, he's under a terrific strain. I can't just suddenly walk in there on him, there's no telling how he might react. Is he a big guy?

BOLTON. Yeah . . . (*He puts down the spray and tries to pull himself together*) Well, I knew it would come to this. You're right. It's my responsibility. (*He paces in anguish*) I should have prepared him for this. Suppose he doesn't feel protective enough? Suppose he doesn't have the right stuff in him after all? (*He stops, thinking desperately*) There must be something I can say to this boy. Everything I think of sounds so phony. He shouldn't have to do this by himself. (WALTER *bursts out of the room and freezes at the sight of* STAN. BOLTON, *suddenly confronted by* WALTER, *drops all attempt at logic and plunges ahead by instinct*) This is my

129

old friend Stan . . . he's an obstetrician . . . (WALTER *stares.* BOLTON *snatches up his book of verse*) He digs your work . . .

WALTER. (*Stares at* BOLTON, *then says quietly to him*) I could use some help.

STAN. I'll be right with you, Walt. Go tell her not to push. (WALTER *dashes back into the room.* STAN *crosses to the stove. He pours the water out of the pot with the instruments, pausing to explain to* BOLTON) You see, I'll just . . .

BOLTON. (*Shrieking in near hysteria*) Will you get in there for Christ's sake?! (*He almost chases* STAN *into the room.* STAN *exits, closing the door.*)

(*An instant too late*)

Hey, don't you want my sheets?!

(WINN *crosses to phone.* BOLTON *crosses to delivery-room door and listens*)

WINN. (*Warmly*) Well! Congratulations, sir, you handled it beautifully! (*Dials*) The use of that word "dig" was just right.

BOLTON. (*Still slightly dazed, and still holding* WALTER'*s book of verse he absently hugs it to his chest and says vaguely*) "Dig?" Did I say that?

WINN. They respond to that sort of thing. (*His call comes through and he speaks into the phone*) Hello, this is Winston Garand. I'd like to speak to Mr. Arlington, please.

BOLTON. (*Snapping to*) Arlington?! (WINN *is nodding.* BOLTON *crosses toward him*) What are you calling him for?!

WINN. (*Covering the mouthpiece*) He's been worried about you. And after what you've just been through, you deserve to hear this. (*Into phone*) Oh, hello, Arthur. Well, we're out of the woods . . . Yes, the doctor is with her now so it's his responsibility now. We're clean . . . Oh, yes, I've stayed with it all along . . . Well, he handled it beautifully, he came up with one of their key words at the crucial moment . . . "dig" . . . yes . . . what? (*Looks across at the bottle of Scotch*) No, he's hardly touched it . . . Yes, I'll tell him . . . Oh, you're welcome, Arthur. Good night. (*He hangs up and turns to* BOLTON, *who is staring at him in shock*) Well, he sends his heartiest congratulations, and I'd like to add mine, too, sir. (*He crosses to counter and picks up bottle*)

BOLTON. Uh, thank you . . . Well, as I said before, Winn, you have a great future.

WINN. (*Crosses to table with bottle*) Thank you, sir. (*He starts to put the bottle of Scotch in his attaché case and then he gets an idea*) Say, why don't I just leave this here? It goes on the swindle sheet anyway.

BOLTON. (*Somehow keeping the anger from his voice*) I'd appreciate that, Winn, since I apparently have a reputation to uphold.

WINN. (*Smiling patronizingly*) We aren't really worried about you, sir.

BOLTON. (*Smiling enigmatically*) Likewise.

WINN. Say, I have a thought: I've got the bill for the Scotch, so why don't you peel off the tax stamp, and we'll both deduct it.

BOLTON. (*Automatically*) Oh, fine. It all adds up, you know.

WINN. Right! (*He starts to leave*) Well, I guess that wraps it . . .

BOLTON. There's one minor correction you might want to make in your report to the president: the key word wasn't "dig," it was "work."

WINN. Oh, really! Well, I'll have to remember that. Thank you. Good night.
(*Polite, pleasant, and smiling to the end, he exits.*)

(BOLTON *closes the door, gives his head a shake as if to clear it, and then runs to the delivery-room door. He listens, but apparently hears nothing significant. He crosses to the table, pours some Scotch into his glass and downs it. Then, still absorbed with thoughts of* DORIS, *he absently takes his expense-account book out of his shirt pocket, and starts to peel the tax stamp off the Scotch. Then, in a sudden wave of revulsion, he savagely rips the expense-account book and hurls it from him. Sitting, he opens* WALTER's *book and after a moment, begins to sing softly to himself*)

BOLTON. . . . . I put my IBM card in that ole pianola and it played out my whole life song . . . (WALTER *bursts out of the room.* BOLTON *snaps the book shut.* WALTER *is too upset to notice*) What's the matter! What happened!

WALTER. (*Almost in tears*) He gave her a shot! She's going to miss it!

BOLTON. Miss what?!

WALTER. Seeing the birth! Gee, she wanted to so much.

BOLTON. But is she going to be all right?!

WALTER. He said she would. She's resting now. (*Pause*) He wants two of your sheets.

BOLTON. (*Thrilled, leaps into action*) Oh! Well! Let's see now . . . (*He can't figure out how to get a sheet down without contaminating it. He panics*) I can't get them down!

WALTER. I'll help you. Just touch the corners. We'll fold them.

BOLTON. Careful now!

(*They each take a corner and fold toward each other. They find themselves face to face*)

WALTER. (*After a pause*) Thanks.

BOLTON. That's all right.

WALTER. (*He accidentally steps on* BOLTON'S *torn-up expense book*) Oh, I . . . (WALTER *looks questioningly at* BOLTON)

BOLTON. Thanks.

WALTER. (*Smiling*) That's all right.

(*Suddenly there is the cry of a newborn baby*)

(WALTER *is stunned*) That's the baby! *I missed it too!*

BOLTON. Oh. (*Crosses to* WALTER *and puts his hand on his shoulder and says sympathetically*) Well, maybe some day you and Doris can . . .

WALTER. (*Interrupting excitedly*) That's right! You know, I never thought of that! (*He whirls around and goes running into the room shouting*) Hey, Doris! Let's have another baby!

GENERATION

(BOLTON *crosses to the door after him. It is closed. He listens for a moment to his grandchild, then sits slowly on a bench by the door, bemused and smiling*)

THE CURTAIN FALLS

13